A SAD DEPARTURE

A SAD DEPARTURE

Why we could not stay in the Church of Scotland

David J. Randall

'You have exalted above all things your name and your word' (Psalm 138:2).

THE BANNER OF TRUTH TRUST

THE BANNER OF TRUTH TRUST
3 Murrayfield Road, Edinburgh EH12 6EL, UK
P.O. Box 621, Carlisle, PA 17013, USA

*

Reprinted 2016

ISBN
Print: 978 1 84871 661 2
Epub: 978 1 84871 663 6
Kindle: 978 1 84871 664 3

*

Typeset in 10/14 pt Sabon Oldstyle Figures at
The Banner of Truth Trust, Edinburgh

Printed in the USA by
Versa Press, Inc.
East Peoria, IL

Contents

Abbreviations:

Kirk: Scottish word for Church
APC: Associated Presbyterian Churches
IPC: International Presbyterian Church
Free Church: The Free Church of Scotland
UF: United Free Church
KJV: King James (or Authorised) Version
NIV: New International Version

Foreword

IF you care at all about the Christian church you must brace yourself for a roller coaster of emotions as you read *A Sad Departure*.

The title contains a *double entendre*. On the one hand it alludes to the departure from the Church of Scotland of about forty ministers and many members. On the other hand it refers to the catalyst of these actions – the departure of the Kirk from its moorings in the authority of Scripture by its decisions on 'the gay question'. Those who have loved and served (and may still be serving) the Church of Scotland, or who feel indebted to its history, will read these pages with a sense of sadness. Other observers, perhaps familiar with the past century and a half of the story of the Church of Scotland, will no doubt feel that the seeds of decisions recorded here were sown in the field many decades ago, even if the crop that is now being harvested could scarcely have been foreseen.

A foreword is meant to introduce and commend a book and not to steal its thunder. But it is always helpful to know something about a book's author—and in this instance some of that knowledge will set what follows in its proper context.

I have known of and observed David Randall for some forty years, although it is only in the last couple of years that we have come to know each other. From a distance he always seemed to be the epitome of a deeply committed, Christ-centred, congregation-loving, faithfully-teaching, Church of Scotland minister. He has that combination of intelligence, seriousness, and graciousness that would have made him a good candidate for featuring as the beloved local minister in one of the old Scottish novels. To reach back further into the literary past, I suspect his congregation could say of him what Chaucer wrote of the 'poor parson of a town': 'Christ's love and his apostles twelve he taught, but first he followed it himself.' For nearly forty years he served the same congregation in Macduff, teaching God's word, and modelling for them Christian living and Christian family life. Feeding his flock and seeking the lost seemed to be the only 'preferment' he sought. All this has simply been confirmed, and indeed enhanced, by coming to know him personally in recent years. It is evident that he has had a deep commitment to, affection for, and desire to serve in, the Church of Scotland in which he was reared – but from which he has now made *a sad departure.*

David Randall is not, then, a hot-headed, division-creating, young rebel. He is rather a man whose record of humble and fruitful service, matched by very few, has, as they say, 'earned him the right to be heard'.

A Sad Departure tells a dark story, almost novelesque in character. A church's Theological Commission reaches a unanimous conclusion on the teaching on marriage given in its ultimate authority, the Bible. But then its General Assembly acts in a way that ignores, demeans, and rejects that teaching. Thus behind these sad departures lies the prior and much sadder departure of the Kirk from its sacred constitution. What John Roberts, Chief Justice of the Supreme Court of the United States, noted in his written dissent from his Court's 2015 decision on marriage, could equally be applied here: the Church of Scotland's highest court has made decisions not on the basis of her ultimately authoritative documents but simply on the basis of the will of the majority of decision-makers.

What makes this *unnerving* in a professing Christian Church is in part the spectre of a lack of integrity that haunts the narrative. (Had ordination vows been made with some impatience or even disdain with respect to their content, and with fingers crossed behind the back?) But what makes it so *staggering* is that the Church of Scotland has for all practical purposes declared herself and not Scripture to be the ultimate authority in a matter of both faith and life. Now *vox Ecclesiae Scotticanae, vox Dei* – the voice of the Church of Scotland is the voice of God!

When the human founders of the Church of Scotland reformed, the famous six Johns, wrote the great Scots Confession of 1560, they prefaced their work by saying that if anyone disagreed with its contents they would answer them 'out of the mouth of God'. From this historic position the present Kirk has removed herself by a whole diameter. Effectively she has turned to Scripture to say 'shut *your* mouth; it is *our* voice, the voice of the contemporary church, which is the voice of God'.

The decisions of the General Assembly of the Kirk have been made with ceremonial dignity and solemnity. There is talk of unity, of working together, of the broad church. All is suffused with the language of 'grace' (although, as some have found, when the issue turns to buildings and finances the language of grace immediately turns to the language of law). But grace can never be found without truth, and Grace Incarnate affirmed that God's word is truth (John 17:17). To demean or refuse it then is a grace-less act.

This then is the story that David Randall chronicles for us here in detail. It is not told with rancour; it is certainly not told by someone who either believes in or seeks out a 'perfect church,' as has been suggested (an historically cheap comment that has always reflected poorly on those who have made it).

Perhaps the 'power-players' in the Kirk have had a quiet and even in some instances cynical confidence that one of the traits of evangelicals is to huff and to puff, but, because of other considerations, remain in the house rather than blow it down. If so then it seems safe to assume that one of the next evangelical boundary markers the Assembly will seek to remove will be the Confession of Faith. Again heroic exertions to retain it may be made. The problem is—and what a painful one it must be for many ministers—'if the foundations are destroyed, what can the righteous do?' (Psa. 11:3). The answer may well be in many instances, 'We do not know; we wish we did.'

True, those who have left the Church of Scotland are certainly in the minority in the way they have answered this question. They have done so one by one, many at great personal cost. But in doing so they have seen with fresh eyes that there is in fact a vibrant church in Scotland outside of the Church of Scotland. Thankfully many of them are now settled in new ministries, some with large numbers of their former congregations who have shared their convictions. But *A Sad Departure* also touches on major concerns that linger in the hearts of many who have remained within the Church of Scotland. As these pages will make clear even the present *status quo* cannot remain for long. For while the Kirk dwarfs other Presbyterian and independent churches in Scotland, already it seems the majority of those who sense themselves called to the ministry of the gospel in Scotland are going elsewhere. The number of evangelical candidates (on whom in the past half century the Church of Scotland has been statistically heavily dependent) is now tiny. The new generation no longer feels the sense of loyalty to the Kirk that mine did; it sees no reason to be loyal to the biblically disloyal. The result will surely be, as the years pass, fewer and fewer congregations will be able to call a minister in the mould of a David Randall.

Thus the key question cannot be reduced to: 'What should we do now?' It must include 'What of the future?' Those who have left may seem small in congregational size, few in number, in some instances without permanent buildings of their own, and much despised. But the issue raised by *A Sad Departure* is in part this: Is it not better to be all that and free now to teach and apply God's word *and build for the future* than to undergo a slow but progressive deterioration through the kind of famine of hearing the words of the Lord that Amos described (Amos 8:11-12)? For at the end of the day unless God's word can be *applied* as well as *taught* the church withers. Famines of hearing the words of the Lord tend to come progressively not suddenly, often because although taught the word of God has not been digested and applied. Where limits are placed on the application of God's word, people become accustomed to meagre diets and begin to regard them as normal; they do not realise they are starving until it is too late. And then the day comes when they realise they need food but no longer know where it can be found.

A Sad Departure is a thoughtful, honest and solemnising book written out of a deep personal and pastoral concern for the cause of the gospel. It cannot have been easy to write. But in its own way it is a heart cry that God would raise up leaders in Scotland like those from Issachar, 'men who had understanding of the times, to know what Israel ought to do'. As in David's day much could be accomplished by '200 chiefs and all their kinsman under their command' (1 Chron. 12:32).

Those who have Scotland's best interests at heart will pray that it may be so.

SINCLAIR B. FERGUSON
September 2015

I

Introduction — What's the Problem?

OVER recent years, many ministers, elders, and members of the Church of Scotland have been disturbed by the denomination's movement away from its professed adherence to Holy Scripture as the basis and foundation of its beliefs and decisions. In this book we will look at decisions of recent General Assemblies which have led some people to follow the line of Dietrich Bonhoeffer's vivid metaphor: 'If you board the wrong train, it is no use running along the corridor in the opposite direction.'[1] The train may be rushing along at 90 mph and, if you realise it is going the wrong way, you will not accomplish much by running back along the corridor in the other direction at, say, 5 mph. You are still on a train that is careering along in the wrong direction.

In the following chapters we will evaluate certain decisions of the General Assembly in light of the Bible's teaching. We will also try to understand the current situation within its historical context, as well as provide a record of the experiences and testimonies of some people who have made a sad departure from the Church of Scotland.

The title of this book, *A Sad Departure*, has a double meaning. It refers to the sadness of those who have decided to leave the Church of Scotland, but it also points to the sad reality of the denomination's departure (through its decision-making body, the General Assembly) from submission to the authority of Scripture.

It was in May 2009 that the General Assembly of the Church of Scotland decided that it was in order for an Aberdeen congregation

[1] E. Metaxas, *Bonhoeffer* (Nelson, 2010), 187.

to proceed with a call to a minister who was living in a homosexual relationship with another man.

The Presbytery of Aberdeen had sustained the call,[1] and subsequently some members of that Presbytery appealed to the General Assembly to over-turn the decision. The Assembly voted by 326 to 267 to uphold the Presbytery's decision. It is sometimes claimed that, even allowing for widespread nominalism in the membership of the Church of Scotland, the General Assembly is unrepresentative and more liberal than the Church as a whole, but it is the Assembly that determines the course of the denomination. It is there that ultimate human authority lies and, whether people like it or not, decisions taken at the Assembly define the position of the Church of Scotland.

This decision has been confirmed by subsequent Assemblies, and the fall-out has been considerable – as was to be expected, since it represents a clear departure from the attitude to the Bible that has been professed by the denomination, as well as by the worldwide church, over the centuries. It is this question of the position and authority of the Bible in the Church that is at the heart of the present controversy. The secular press often represents the dispute as a struggle over whether the Church should be 'pro-gay' or 'anti-gay', but the basic issue is that of the relationship of the Church to the Bible.

The story is told of a multi-storey office-building where cracks appeared in a wall on the forty-second floor.[2] The managing director sent for an architect to come and investigate. He took the elevator to the forty-second floor to meet the architect but couldn't find him. Eventually the architect was located in the basement. The managing director remonstrated with him: 'What are you doing down here – we have a serious problem on the forty-second floor.' The architect's answer was: 'You may have cracks on the forty-second floor, but your problem is not on the forty-second

[1] A procedure whereby a Presbytery agrees that there is no hindrance to a proposed induction.

[2] Recounted by Charles Price in article in *Decision* magazine, January 1990.

floor; your problem is down here in the basement.' It later came to light that a janitor was building a garage at home and every evening he chiselled out one brick from the wall, put it in his bag and took it home. After several years, cracks appeared high up on the forty-second floor!

The story illustrates what has been happening in the Church of Scotland for a number of years. The 'crack on the forty-second floor' is the crisis that has been occasioned by the question of the rightness or wrongness of inducting practising homosexual people to the Christian ministry, but the real problem is down in the foundations, where liberally-minded people have been chiselling away at the biblical foundations of the Church for a long time.

That is going to be the main thesis of this book as we record the withdrawal of many from the Church of Scotland because of its refusal to uphold the teaching of God's word. Our concern will be to emphasise what the Bible says on the particular issue before the Church, but also (and more importantly) we will major on the underlying question of the authority of the Bible in the life of the Church. Why does it matter what the Bible teaches? That 'problem of authority has always been crucial in the life of the individual and the Church; and to Protestants that authority has always been found in the Lord Jesus Christ Himself mediated to us through "the infallible Word." The Bible and our attitude to it has always therefore been at the very heart and centre of the conflict between ... liberal and modernistic Protestantism.'[1]

In seeking to record what has happened, we do not intend to be disrespectful to anyone – homosexual people, people who experience same-sex attraction, the Church of Scotland, the General Assembly, or evangelicals who believe it right to stay in the Church of Scotland. Several things may be emphasised at the outset:

- Those who have left the Church of Scotland have not been, and are not, enemies of the Church of Scotland; we hope that the

[1] D. M. Lloyd-Jones in foreword: *The Infallible Word, Westminster Seminary Symposium* (Philadelphia: Presbyterian & Reformed Publishing, 1946), ix.

word 'sad' in the title conveys that. Our intention is to provide an account of what has happened, with some explanation. As one former Church of Scotland minister (formerly convener of one of the Church's major boards) has written, 'A sad departure? Yes but the sadness was not really in having to leave the denomination with which many of us had been associated for decades. The sadness rather continues to be in the departure of that denomination from the one holy, catholic and apostolic faith.' We will seek to be clear on the issues, but hopefully it is possible to be straightforward without being disrespectful and to disagree without being disagreeable.

• The same applies to our attitude to homosexual people; there is no justification for bigotry or so-called 'gay-bashing'. Jesus teaches that we should love our neighbour, which, along with love to God, is the summation of the commandments (Matt. 22:37-40).

• Thirdly, we have no desire to aggravate the differences of view that have arisen within the evangelical constituency. This book is written from the point of view of those who have departed, and we shall pose some questions for those evangelicals who advocate remaining within the denomination, but we must also recognise and accept that there has not been unanimity among evangelical ministers, elders, and members over the issue.

• And it should also be emphasised that we are not talking about a departure or withdrawal from 'the church'. The 'holy catholic church' of the Apostles' Creed is the international and inter-generational fellowship of those who put their trust in Jesus Christ and seek to follow him.[1] Our departure from the Church

[1] The Scots Confession of 1560, drawn up by John Knox and others (ed. William Croft Dickinson, vol. 2, p. 266) says, 'It is a thing most requisite that the true Kirk be discerned by clear and perfect notes.' Such notes are said to be not 'antiquity, title usurped, lineal descent, place appointed, nor multitude of men approving an error', but 'First, The true preaching of the Word of God; into the which God has revealed himself to us, as the writings of the Prophets and Apostles do declare. Secondly, The right administration of the sacraments of Christ Jesus ... Last, Ecclesiastical discipline, uprightly ministered, as God's Word prescribes. Wheresoever these former notes are seen, and of any time continue (be the number never so few above two or three) there is the true Kirk of Christ.'

of Scotland does not entail an abandonment of 'the church of God, which he obtained with his own blood' (Acts 20:28), the community of faith 'built on the foundation of the apostles and prophets, Christ Jesus himself being the cornerstone, in whom the whole structure, being joined together grows into a holy temple in the Lord' (Eph. 2:20-21).

Sadness and Excitement

Alongside the sadness that is felt by many in these days there is also a sense of excitement. The fall-out from Assembly decisions has caused a shake-up in many quarters, and we are witnessing a re-alignment of the Christian church in Scotland. New churches and new ministries are developing and it is going to be exciting to see what Almighty God will bring out of the turmoil.

One of the endeavours to persuade members not to depart from the Church of Scotland[1] has suggested that, in light of what its author calls 'this shameful decision' (namely, to allow the training and ordination of practising homosexual men and woman as ministers of Word and Sacrament in the Church of Scotland), it may merely soothe our consciences and ease our pain to leave the Church of Scotland. This is simply not so; leaving the denomination has *caused* us pain – although many have also testified to a sense of relief and release upon their departure.

It is not that any of the ministers, members, and congregations who have sadly left the Church of Scotland have done so with any assumption that they can find or found a *perfect* church. A correspondent to the Church of Scotland magazine, *Life & Work*, referred to the 2014 Moderator's remarks at the close of the Assembly that year, in which he addressed those who had left or were contemplating leaving: 'Let us know when you have settled in the perfect church and we will come round and inspect its credentials.' Such unworthy remarks are far wide of the mark. The letter-writer, who had already left the denomination, described the

[1] Letter by the Moderator of the Presbytery of Uist, August 2014.

Moderator's words as unpleasant and surprising. He suggested that the Moderator 'knows better than most that people like me are not leaving the Church of Scotland in search of the perfect church. Rather it is because we know that, whether it is a nation, a church or a human heart, God will only honour his truth, and we believe that the Church of Scotland has now clearly departed from that truth ... we seek not a new church or a broad church or a narrow church or a modern church but a faithful church.'[1]

In his Second Letter to the Corinthians the apostle Paul wrote, 'What we proclaim is not ourselves, but Jesus Christ as Lord, with ourselves as your servants for Jesus' sake.' He then went on, 'But we have this treasure in jars of clay, to show that the surpassing power belongs to God and not to us' (2 Cor. 4:5-7). Those who have left the Church of Scotland do not claim to be 'better' or 'holier' than anyone else; it is simply a matter of seeking to be faithful to what God has revealed and what we believe to be his guidance.

In chapter 4 we will discuss the arguments of evangelicals who believe that the right thing to do is to remain within the Church of Scotland. Among reasons for staying are:

• the belief that it is evangelicals who are 'the real Church of Scotland'. Why, they would ask, should *we* leave? Shouldn't it be the liberals who leave the denomination?

• the view that, if the denomination has moved from its true foundations, evangelicals should work from within to restore it.

• the assertion that Scotland has had too many divisions and schisms, and we should strive for unity.

• the recourse to the parochial view that, so long as 'they' leave me alone to exercise a biblical and evangelical ministry within my parish, there is no need to leave.

• the responsibility to care for the people in the parish to which

[1] Brian McDowell in letter to *Life & Work*, August 2014.

I was called – caring for believers and reaching out to the secular society around us.

• a desire to be part of a national church, with all the pastoral and evangelistic opportunities that this has afforded and may still afford.

This book, as well as seeking to provide a record of recent events, sets forward the view of those who believe that, significant as the above points are, they are outweighed by the seriousness of the denomination's departure from its scriptural basis.

So far as this author is concerned, I write as one who has had some degree of involvement in the controversies of the last few years. When the Special Commission appointed by the General Assembly of 2009 planned to produce a DVD for meetings of Kirk Sessions and Presbyteries, I was invited to represent the so-called 'traditionalist view',[1] as opposed to 'the revisionist view' expressed by another minister. I also took part in several media interviews and in debates at Presbytery and Assembly level.

I write with a sense of personal sadness since I owe much to the Church of Scotland. It has been part of my familial DNA. My grandfather and father were elders of the Church of Scotland and I was brought up within its fellowship and worship. I served as a minister of Word and Sacrament for four decades in which I sought to serve my parish and also take an active part in Presbytery life and Assembly boards and committees. It has been with great reluctance that I have concluded that it was right to depart from the denomination for the reasons which are explored within these pages. The decline of the Church of Scotland in these last few decades, culminating in decisions of recent General Assemblies, is nothing less than tragic, and it is only with great sorrow that I and many others have concluded that we must leave.

Anecdotally, I recall the case of a congregation (Gardenstown) many years ago that was being urged to secede from the Church

[1] The word 'traditionalist' will be used several times in these pages (since it has been widely used in the relevant reports), but it is a misnomer; it is not tradition but Scripture that determines what evangelicals believe.

of Scotland because the denomination was alleged to be moving in the direction of approval of homosexual practice. I, along with the Rev. James Philip (the then minister of Holyrood Abbey Church in Edinburgh), spoke at a congregational meeting, urging members to resist secession and remain with the denomination.

This illustrates the way in which some of us have tried very hard to work within the Church of Scotland and even to defend it against its detractors; personally, I once suggested to an Assembly official that for the Church of Scotland to lose my support was a remarkable achievement! Many others could say the same thing, and our love for the Church of Scotland makes ours a very reluctant and sad exodus.

In his closing address to the 2014 General Assembly, the Moderator challenged the Theological Forum to 'reframe the Church's doctrinal standards in order to understand better the acceptable boundaries of what might be called the theological pluralism which is the Church of Scotland.' This latter phrase is a remarkable one to be used by the Moderator of a confessional church such as the Church of Scotland. It may be regrettable that some Scottish communities have congregations of four or five different Presbyterian denominations,[1] and it would be wonderful if they would come together, but if they ever do so, it will not be in the name of some kind of theological pluralism!

People sometimes speak about an evangelical wing of the Church and there has been vague talk of how the Church of Scotland might move towards the recognition of itself as a combination of different 'wings', one of which would be the evangelical wing. South of the border, the Church of England is often described as a broad church, and one former Anglican vicar tells of the remark of a bishop which might seem amusing but which is nevertheless poignant. He was meeting with some evangelical clergy in his diocese, and the evangelicals were emphasising biblical truths about the one way of salvation through the sacrificial death of Christ. They admitted that they could learn from others, but as

[1] There are said to be eleven Presbyterian denominations in Scotland.

for salvation, they said, there is only one way (cf. Acts 4:12). The bishop's response was, 'Thank you. I do hope you'll go on making your particular contribution'![1]

Various groupings of evangelicals within the Church of Scotland *have* been formed, which may have been necessary and helpful, but that is very different from an acceptance of the notion that the Church should be regarded as an umbrella denomination under which evangelicals should content themselves with being one of several 'wings'. Not all would go so far as one former Moderator who characterised certain evangelicals as 'grumbling grunters' and 'a few oddballs out on the extremities of the Church', but it is odd that in a denomination that claims to recognise the word of God as its supreme rule of faith and life and the Westminster Confession as its subordinate standard, evangelicals could content themselves with being a wing of a pluralistic Church.

After the 2014 General Assembly, the Rev. Jeremy Middleton, Chairman of the Crieff Fellowship, referred to the Moderator's closing address in which he described the Assembly week as 'a momentous week in the life of our Church'. Sharing that assessment, though for very different reasons, Mr Middleton suggested,

> Through the course of that week of General Assembly, the Church of Scotland carefully re-defined herself as an essentially liberal denomination – a denomination which now has, it would seem (for all the rhetoric), little time for, and little truck with, those who adhere to a thoroughly biblical position. The 'name-calling' in the early part of the week may have been an unfortunate slip of the tongue, but it was surely revealing.

Liberals often assert that the things that unite us are greater than the things that divide us, but if we are divided on the question of scriptural authority and whether we adhere to God's teaching there, then we are seriously divided.

The question may be raised as to whether it is perhaps too early to attempt a review of this kind. Some of us have been close to

[1] Reg Burrows, *Dare to Contend* (Jude Publications, 1990), 13.

the heart of the battle and it is still very recent history. *Are* we too close to the events? In response it might be said that, although the particular context is contemporary (we are, after all, considering things that, even thirty years ago, would have been regarded as inconceivable), the issue of loyalty to denomination as against scriptural faithfulness is by no means a new issue. It has faced people at various times and in various contexts. Moreover, it will hopefully be helpful to record some of the story of the present conflict before, with the passage of time, issues become blurred and people begin to forget what happened and why.

We have spoken above about a combination of sadness and excitement, and it is with a positive sense of excitement that this account has been put together. If it is true that man's extremity is God's opportunity,[1] then we may look for good things from the hand of God, because, although we certainly live in a difficult time and although we deserve only judgment, God is gracious and nothing is too hard for him (Jer. 32:17).

Secularism

It is obviously true that secularism has been tightening its grip on British society in recent years and there is a growing intolerance toward Christian commitment and evangelism. Our governments crossed a line when they decided to re-define marriage so that two men or two women may 'marry' one another. This marked a decisive and deliberate break with Judaeo-Christian beliefs and values – and in the case of the Prime Minister, David Cameron, is strangely inconsistent with his insistence that 'Britain is a Christian country and atheists should get over it'!

This 'redefinition' has delighted those who want to rid our society of Christian influence and biblical values, but the Prime Minister's remarks have irked them greatly. As an editorial in a Solas newsletter[2] said, 'No sooner had the Prime Minister referred

[1] Attributed to John Flavel (1627–91).

[2] http://www.solas-cpc.org/wp/wp-content/uploads/2014/09/SolasInsightSept2014.pdf.

to Britain as a Christian country (leaving aside the question of what he understands Christianity to be) than a bevy of atheists were up in arms, suggesting that he was fostering social division and alienation.'

There have been many high-profile cases of action being taken against Christians who have had the temerity to take an open stand on some matter or other. One of the most recent of many examples concerns a senior occupational therapist who was summoned to appear before a disciplinary hearing and found guilty of three 'offences': praying for a newly-qualified Muslim colleague (who had consented to being prayed for), inviting her to a church charity event, and giving her a Christian book. According to *Evangelical Times* which reported the case, 'The ruling against the senior therapist was made despite the fact that the complainant failed to attend the disciplinary hearing and one of the witnesses had said he was pressured into making statements against her.'

There have been many such instances of the attempt to silence Christians and eliminate Christian influence, and it is clear that Christian mission and evangelism are difficult in an increasingly secular, materialistic, and pluralistic culture (a culture rather like the one in which the gospel first took root and began to expand).

In 1974, J. I. Packer wrote of British national life, 'We are no longer publicly pro-Christian, but we are not yet publicly anti-Christian either.'[1] How times have changed! Great Britain is 'officially' a Christian country, and surveys show that the majority of people consider Christianity to be their religion; at the same time, however, there has developed the kind of anti-Christian momentum which has been illustrated above. The census figures may say that atheists constitute a minority of the British population, but it is clear that there are many who may *say* they consider themselves Christians but *live* as practical atheists. In the forty-plus years since Packer made his assertion, much has changed. Today there is a kind of anti-Christian 'political correctness', and we can

[1] Reported in *Third Way*, April 1977.

only hope – and pray – that people will eventually wake-up to the absurdity of many aspects of contemporary social mores and the barrenness of atheistic secularism.

Reflecting on these mores, Melanie Phillips has written:

> Multiculturalism became the orthodoxy of the day, along with non-judgmentalism and lifestyle choice. The only taboo now was the expression of normative majority values such as monogamy, heterosexuality, Christianity or Britishness.[1]

She has elsewhere referred to such events as the forced resignation of a registrar who refused to officiate at a same-sex Civil Partnership ceremony, and the closure of adoption agencies which refuse to place children with homosexual couples, and:

> In Britain, the anti-discrimination orthodoxy has led to a systematic campaign against Christians – particularly over the issue of homosexuality, the key area where Christians run up against social libertarianism in the public square. Freedom of conscience, the cardinal tenet of a liberal society, has been swept aside in the cause of gay rights. While true prejudice against homosexuals or anyone else is reprehensible, 'prejudice' has been redefined to include the expression of normative values.[2]

Much of our contemporary culture (at least of its media and political leaders) has accepted the equivalence of homosexual relationships and now same-sex 'marriage'. Within less than fifty years we have come from a situation in Britain where homosexual practice was a crime to a situation where it is regarded as a crime to think it strange, unnatural or, worst of all, sinful – so that in a recent radio programme the interviewer responded to a lesbian's comment about people asking her about her sexuality, by saying, in tones of incredulity, 'Even yet?' Those who will not toe the line are disparaged as intolerant, judgemental, homophobic dinosaurs.

[1] *Londonistan* (Gibson Square, 2006), 65.
[2] *The World Turned Upside Down* (Encounter, 2010), 101.

Conformed or Transformed?

If such a change is remarkable in society, it is also remarkable that, within a Church that professes to stand on the teaching of the Bible and belief in Jesus Christ, there should be such a departure from long-accepted Christian values as has been seen in recent years. If the aforementioned change in social attitudes within a short space of time is remarkable, it is even more remarkable that within the wider church people scarcely raise an eyebrow when someone questions the Virgin Birth or resurrection of Christ. But it is a different matter if someone has the temerity to imply that homosexual practice is sinful![1] Have we forgotten the apostolic word: 'Do not be conformed to this world, but be transformed by the renewal of your mind, that by testing you may discern what is the will of God, what is good and acceptable and perfect'? (Romans 12:2).

In terms of numerical strength and social influence, it was in the 1950s that the Church of Scotland reached its height. I was eleven years old when the statistics for 1956 recorded that the Church of Scotland had more than 1.25 million members and 2,200 congregations (mostly single charges with their own minister). I grew up in a time when the streets were quiet on Sundays and few public events were held on the Christian Sabbath. Sunday Schools were thriving; I remember seeing three double-decker buses with streamers flying from the windows as they transported one Sunday School on its annual summer picnic. Schools and churches worked in tandem, church services were broadcast on television, and the General Assembly was a huge event for the nation's media. Now, in 2015, the Church of Scotland has fewer than 400,000 members and has approximately 800 ministers serving 1,400 congregations. The decline has been relentless and, as the Principal of Trinity

[1] As recently as 1997, David F. Wright wrote, 'The cohesiveness of a body like the Church of Scotland will surely be tested as never before – if (which God forbid) it tolerates elders living together outside marriage or practising homosexuals pairing off in the manse.' *Truth and Love in a Sexually Disordered World* (Paternoster, 1997), 26.

College, Glasgow has remarked, 'Most people in the Kirk, along with most ministers, are unlikely to have had the experience of being part of a growing congregation.'[1]

It is sad to record such facts and there are no easy explanations of the reasons for such decline. No doubt many social and lifestyle factors play their part, but the tragedy is that in many ways the Church, in seeking to 'move with the times', has itself contributed to the decline, despite many schemes designed to reverse the trend – reappraisals for mission, urgent calls, *etc.* For many years the decline was attributed to the dropping-off of 'dead wood', people who had become members of the Church without any real commitment to Christ. It was once possible to be consoled by the thought of a leaner and fitter Church, but today the Church of Scotland is losing many strongly committed believers and financial supporters.

A few years ago, a Member of Parliament made comment on the Church of England's then decision to reject the introduction of women bishops; he said that if the Church of England wanted to be a national church, it would have to reflect the values of the nation. This is in stark contrast to the words of Romans 12:2 which exhort the Christian church *not* to follow the world's agenda. The church's prime responsibility is to be true to its Master and what he has caused to be written down. As for moving with the times – when the times are moving away from God and his truth, then it would be disloyal and disastrous to move with them!

The late David F. Wright[2] expressed the view that much of the pressure for the church to revise its teaching on marriage and sexuality had sprung from 'a concern (or fear) that the Church will otherwise find itself increasingly out of touch with society at large.' As an instance of this kind of concern, he wrote,

> Witness the extraordinary weight given in the General Assembly in 1994 by a convenor of the Panel on Doctrine to the statistic

[1] Dr Doug Gay, in *Life & Work*, October 2014.

[2] *The Kirk: National or Christian?* in *The Realm of Reform*, ed. R. D. Kernohan (Handsel Press, 1999), 36.

that 99% of a certain age group had had sex before marriage. How unthinkable, so the implication went, that the Church of the nation should maintain unaltered its conviction that sex outside marriage was invariably wrong. Who wants to belong to such a tiny minority? How can it alone claim to be right?

If it is the case, as reported in a 2015 survey (of 1,300 churchgoers)[1] that two-thirds of those polled said that their views on sexuality had become more 'inclusive' in the last ten years, are we simply to conclude, 'Oh well, then, if churchgoers are changing their minds, that settles it'? Are our attitudes to be decided by majority vote? Are we to go along the line of the villagers who, according to Rudyard Kipling, once voted that the earth is flat?[2] Are we to take the line of some political parties which were savaged in the United Kingdom's General Election of 2015 and have concluded that they need to make drastic changes to win back the support of the electorate? Or should we not echo the words of Balaam: 'Though Balak were to give me his house full of silver and gold, I could not go beyond the command of the LORD my God to do less or more' (Num. 22:18)?

Naturally people like to be liked. That is true of institutions as well as individuals, but what if the cost is too high? What if the cost of acceptance with the world is the compromise of revealed truth? Or, in more familiar words, what profit would there be in gaining the whole world and losing one's soul? (Mark 8:36) Are we really supposed to maintain a socially acceptable role at the cost of our biblical fidelity?

These are undoubtedly difficult days for Christian mission and outreach, and that very fact should throw us back to a greater dependence on God himself. It is 'not by might, nor by power, but by my Spirit, says the LORD of hosts' (Zech. 4:6) that anything is accomplished for his kingdom. The apostle Paul referred to his ministry in Corinth and gave it as his testimony:

[1] Survey undertaken by Oasis Trust and reported in article in *Daily Telegraph*, 20 March 2015, by the Telegraph's religious affairs editor.

[2] G. B. Caird, *The Truth of the Gospel* (Oxford University Press, 1950), 8.

> I was with you in weakness and in fear and much trembling, and my speech and my message were not in plausible words of wisdom, but in demonstration of the Spirit and of power, so that your faith might not rest in the wisdom of men but in the power of God (1 Cor. 2:3-5).

It is surely understandable for a former minister of the parish of Macduff in the north-east of Scotland to refer to the words spoken by the character of that name in Shakespeare's *Macbeth*: 'Stands Scotland where it did?' It is the sad belief of many that, if the question were posed, 'Stands the Church of Scotland where it did?', the answer would have to be a sad 'No.' Through its General Assembly the denomination has moved from its biblical foundations. The context is the question of whether to ordain and induct practising homosexuals to ministry, but the underlying issue is: Do we stand under the authority of the word of God in Scripture, or do we nowadays know better?

When Martin Luther was summoned to the Diet of Worms in 1521, he famously said, 'Unless I am convicted by Scripture and plain reason – I do not accept the authority of popes and councils, for they have contradicted each other – my conscience is captive to the word of God. I cannot and I will not recant anything, for to go against conscience is neither right nor safe. God help me. Amen'[1] – perhaps adding, 'Here I stand. I cannot do otherwise.'

It is easy, and sometimes cheap, for critics to accuse those who have left the Church of Scotland of bigotry and even (strange misnomer) homophobia,[2] or to suggest that evangelical people are obsessed with issues relating to sex and sexuality. Such allegations are false. *We* did not choose this battle or issue any challenge to what had always been regarded as orthodox teaching.

It simply will not do to acknowledge Scripture's authority at points where its teaching matches what, on other grounds, we want to maintain and at the same time ignore, suppress or contradict

[1] Quoted in Roland Bainton, *Here I Stand* (Mentor, 1950), 144.

[2] Presumably when people use the term 'homophobic' they are meaning to refer to dislike or intolerance of homosexual people, but a phobia is a fear, not a dislike, of something.

it where it clashes with our own desires. To go down that road is to believe not in the Bible but in ourselves. When I was a student I heard John Stott say, in the course of the Annual Presidential Address of the New College Missionary Society, that some people use the Bible in the same way as statisticians use statistics, namely as a drunk man uses a lamp post – for support, not illumination!

Crisis or Opportunity?

After the 2009 General Assembly of the Church of Scotland, I wrote a paper entitled, 'Crisis or Opportunity', which was updated after the 2013 Assembly opted for a 'mixed economy' in which individual congregations would be allowed to depart from the historic position of the Church if they so chose. The 2013 wording was:

> affirm the Church's historic and current doctrine and practice in relation to human sexuality; nonetheless permit those Kirk Sessions who wish to depart from that doctrine and practice to do so.

This was presented as a compromise to keep people together within the denomination, but it is patently self-contradictory and absurd. To put matters plainly: if the Church of Scotland is to stand by the 'Church's historic and current doctrine', how can it allow the ordination of practising homosexuals – and if it allows the ordination of practising homosexuals, how can it be said to be holding to the Church's historic and current doctrine? It is comparable to the government reaffirming the speed limit of 30 mph in urban areas, but at the same time allowing those who wish to depart from that ruling to do so.

The title of my General Assembly paper, came from a character in the Chinese alphabet which may represent both crisis and opportunity. The recurring decisions of recent General Assemblies present both a crisis and an opportunity. The mantra of the 'establishment' that 'there is no crisis' only reveals the depth of the crisis facing the Church of Scotland (which was already facing a crisis of manpower and finance before this particular issue arose). Members who accept the authority of Scripture have been placed in a crisis of conscience; how could they remain part of a denomination that has effectively set aside the teaching of the Bible (despite all formal claims that the written word is its supreme rule of faith and life)?

Liberals and so-called traditionalists agree that wherever the Bible refers to homosexual practices it does so negatively, describing them as unnatural and sinful. Bible-believers insist that such scriptural teaching must be decisive for the Church; revisionists believe that, for one reason or another, we can ignore or overlook the Bible's teaching on this matter.

Prior to each Assembly in recent years much prayer has been offered – prayer that the Assembly would turn around and stand by biblical teaching. Many special prayer meetings were held, in addition to the private prayers offered. Does the Assembly's decision lead us to conclude that these prayers were unanswered, or is it clear that they *have been* answered and God is leading biblical Christians away from the Church of Scotland? In simple terms, shouldn't we take 'No' for an answer?

For a long time now liberals within the Church have worked with a complacent expectation that evangelicals would settle down after a while and come to accept such departures from orthodoxy. There are some evangelicals who advocate such a course – accepting that the Church has made a wrong choice but who still hope for a reversal of the decision. Others insist that it is a bridge too far and will not cross it.

But let it be emphasised again that those who have reached the latter conclusion are not enemies of the Church of Scotland. Like many, I owe an enormous debt, under God, to the Church of Scotland. A colleague wrote, 'born and bred in it, I would have defended it to the death!' At one time many of us could never have imagined the thought of leaving the denomination; our love for the Church of Scotland made us very reluctant to depart. Evangelicals, far from being trigger-happy schismatics, have been loyal to an increasingly liberal church for a very long time.

Some evangelicals also need to repent of past attitudes of complacency about the place of the Kirk in Scotland. Once, we entertained the assumption that if God was going to do any great thing in Scotland, he would do it through the Church of Scotland. For some of us it has been a hard struggle to depart from such an 'only-show-in-town' attitude and to realise the principle enshrined in F. W. Boreham's story, 'The Candle and the Bird.' When a candle is extinguished the light goes out, but when a bird is driven away, it simply leaves to sing its song somewhere else.[1]

Some people have argued that the issue is not a dividing issue, but it *is* a fundamental issue: where does authority lie in the church? Is decision-making to be controlled by the word of God in Scripture, as has been believed through the ages – or is it to be controlled by our own wisdom, by contemporary mores or by the kind of social pressure that is strong in our contemporary anti-authoritarian culture?

The issue was highlighted in the correspondence columns of a newspaper[2] in which the writer referred to a congregation whose minister had retired:

> As someone who goes to [the church concerned] twice a month [*sic*], I feel what is needed is someone who can relate to ordinary people like myself, without referring to the Bible.

If that is crass, one may well ask whether it is more or less so than the decisions of the august body known as the General Assembly. The Church of Scotland *professes* belief in the Scriptures as the supreme rule of its faith and life but it has officially (by decision of its supreme court) turned its back on the Bible. After the manner of Genesis 3, doubting God's word has been followed by denial of God's word, and denial of God's word has been followed by defiance of God's word.

Many evangelicals have valiantly tried to be gospel salt in an increasingly liberal Church over a long period. Despite claims to

[1] Quoted in R. Zacharias, *Cries of the Heart* (Word Publishing, 1998), 28.
[2] *Edinburgh Evening News*, 2 June 2014.

the contrary, many have served within the structures of the Church of Scotland and have sought to exert a positive evangelical influence, but sadly their efforts have not affected the general drift into liberalism that has characterised the denomination for many years.

It is sometimes suggested that evangelicals have in the past accepted the breadth of a broad church and have tolerated deviation on the part of many, including ministers, so why depart from such a church now? The answer to that question is that error is now being *promoted* denominationally rather than merely *tolerated* locally. No doubt we have all been complicit in too great an acceptance of error in various forms and a lack of church discipline, but surely there comes a point where we have to say, 'No further.'

A younger colleague made the poignant complaint that he was often encouraged by older evangelicals and always thought they exemplified a 'Bible first' mind-set; but he now wonders if that has now given way to a 'Church of Scotland first' way of thinking for many?

There is no more important issue than that of the authority of the word of God because our belief about the Bible determines our beliefs about everything else. The written word, which centres in the One who became flesh for our salvation, and the living Word are brought together in Psalm 138:2: 'You have exalted above all things your name and your word.' We must strive to honour the name of the Lord *and* the word of the Lord. Jesus himself said, 'Whoever is of God hears the words of God' (John 8:47). On another occasion he warned:

> Whoever is ashamed of me and of my words in this adulterous and sinful generation, of him will the Son of Man also be ashamed when he comes in the glory of his Father with the holy angels (Mark 8:38).

2

Recent General Assemblies

IN coming to a decision about the ordination and/or induction into ministry of people in active homosexual relationships the all-important question ought to be – what does the Bible say? If the view of the world and the view of the Bible clash, then the words of Peter and the apostles in Acts 5:29 must be our rule: 'We must obey God rather than men.' It is easy for our critics to accuse us of anti-gay bigotry. This we reject, but we cannot reject the teaching of Scripture.

Those who have taken a public stand against such inductions have sometimes been asked, 'What would happen if homosexual people came to your church?' – with the implication being that we probably would not allow them through the door! Such a charge is absurd; for a start, services of worship are public events. When noticeboards say, 'All welcome', they mean that. We are all sinners by nature and the Bible's message is for all. 'God so loved the world, that he gave his only Son, that *whoever* believes in him should not perish but have eternal life' (John 3:16). No selection process takes place at the church door on this or any other matter, for the church's belief is in a message of good news. We hold to a gospel that says, 'Whosoever will' may come (Rev. 22:17, KJV) and a Lord who says, 'Whoever comes to me I will never cast out' (John 6:37).

Nevertheless it is in the context of this particular controversy that the present crisis has arisen. The Bible is clear in its teaching about homosexual practice and, that being so, the issue becomes one of biblical authority. Are we to stand by what the Bible says or are we to follow the famous example of American President Thomas Jefferson who took (literal) scissors and paste to the Bible, cutting out whatever was not to his liking in order to produce his book *The Life and Morals of Jesus of Nazareth*?[1]

In this chapter we will outline the events in connection with the last few General Assemblies of the Church of Scotland before turning our attention (in chapter 4) to the question of what the Bible says on the particular matter under consideration. After that, we will proceed to look at the vital issue of why we should pay any heed to what the Bible says.

It should also be borne in mind that the decisions taken have been decisions of the General Assembly – not of '121', the Kirk's headquarters in George Street, Edinburgh. Evangelicals may sometimes imply that it is the ecclesiastical establishment that has made wrong decisions, but these, in fact, have been the persistent wrong decisions of General Assemblies which have, in the typically forthright words of Professor Donald Macleod, concluded that 'the loss of a few thousand obscurantist Evangelicals was a small price to pay' for keeping a minister who 'decided that his personal "right" to a non-biblical lifestyle was more important than the peace of the church'.[2]

Prior to 2009

In 2006 the General Assembly debated the question of whether or not a minister wishing to 'bless' a couple in a homosexual relationship (a Civil Partnership) would be immune from disciplinary proceedings. The Assembly was minded to say that such a minister would not be disciplined, but the Rev. Ian Watson persuaded the Assembly that such a matter should be sent to Presbyteries 'under the Barrier Act'. The Barrier Act is a historic safeguard (since 1697) against spontaneous, sudden, and unexamined changes

[1] Jefferson (1743–1826) did not actually call it a Bible and it was only published some time after his death (1895).

[2] Comment in *West Highland Free Press*, 13 February 2015.

in the Church's doctrine or worship. Under the Act, a proposed alteration has to be sent down for consideration by the Presbyteries and, only if it is approved by the majority of them, can it then be passed into legislation by the following General Assembly. Part of Ian Watson's argument was that when the Assembly decided in the 1950s to allow the remarriage in Church of divorced persons (for which there is at least some scriptural warrant under certain conditions), that change had had to go down under the Barrier Act – how much more should any kind of approval of a homosexual Civil Partnership.[1]

In due course, 36 Presbyteries voted against and 9 for, so that, when this was reported to the General Assembly of 2007, the proposed Act fell.

However, by the end of the following year another matter had arisen.

2009

In November 2008 an Aberdeen congregation voted on whether to issue a call to a minister of another congregation, who was not only divorced from his wife (with whom he had a daughter), but who was also living in an openly homosexual relationship with another man. The congregation concerned voted by 140 to 28 to uphold the call.

This decision then required the approval of the Presbytery of Aberdeen, which voted by 60 to 24 to approve the induction (the admission of a minister to a pastoral charge). Some members of

[1] Articles in *Life & Work* have suggested that the Barrier Act is an antiquated piece of legislation which presents an obstacle to visionary reform and should therefore be repealed. Such articles have not made explicit reference to the subject of Civil Partnerships, but a colleague (Rev. Andrew Coghill) examined the Legislative Acts of Assembly over a period of sixteen years and found that during that time the Barrier Act was employed in relation to nineteen pieces of proposed legislation, most of which were non-controversial. Eighteen of these items passed through Presbyteries more or less 'on the nod'. The *only* one which did not was the one about the blessing of Civil Partnerships. Such a finding (18 out of 19), he suggests, hardly supports the idea that the Barrier Act is an undesirable obstacle to reform.

the Presbytery launched an appeal against this decision, which was heard, first by a Commission of Assembly, and then by the General Assembly itself.

Prior to the meeting of the Assembly, an online petition against such an induction was signed by 12,555 people, including 481 Church of Scotland ministers, 33 Kirk Sessions, over 700 ministers from Protestant and Roman Catholic churches in Great Britain and Ireland, and over 500 ministers serving overseas. However, after a four-hour debate on 23 May 2009, the General Assembly voted by 326 to 267 to uphold the decision of Aberdeen Presbytery. The said induction took place in July of that year.

On the day after the Assembly debate, the *Guardian* reported:

> Senior Church of Scotland traditionalists were furious about the vote, arguing that it created a precedent that authorised the ordination and appointment of gay clergy and 'brought shame' on their church. 'It sends a clear signal to the world that our denomination has departed from the teaching of the Christian Scriptures, upon which its very existence depends. It is a deeply painful day for all who love Christ and his Gospel,' said the Fellowship of Confessing Churches.[1] Two leading conservatives, the Rev. David Court from Edinburgh and the Rev. William Philip from Glasgow ... warned it would alienate many lay members: 'We deeply regret the decision of the General Assembly, which has brought great shame on the name of our Lord Jesus Christ and his church by publicly proclaiming as holy what God, the Bible, and orthodox Christianity all down the ages, and all over the world, unambiguously call sin. This is about far more than just sexuality. The very nature of the Christian gospel is at stake.'

Several meetings were held after that Assembly and various papers were written to affirm the so-called traditionalist view. One such paper suggested that liberals may have expected evangelicals

[1] The Fellowship of Confessing Churches was developed and sponsored by the St George's Tron congregation in Glasgow. The Fellowship proclaimed its rejection of 'new teachings and practices which depart from the historic Christian faith, turn away from the orthodox gospel of repentance and faith, and publicly sanctify what the Bible proclaims as sin'.

to settle down after a while and simply accept the new situation, as had been done, for example, with the unwelcome decision to allow congregations to apply for lottery-funding; conservatives didn't like it but they had to accept that that decision had been made. However it was argued that the new situation was of a different order and that, notwithstanding any attempt to gag people,[1] evangelicals would not just roll over and accept what they would regard as biblically unacceptable.

In my paper, 'Crisis or Opportunity?', written after the 2009 Assembly, I sought to underline several important considerations arising from that year's controversies:

1. The first was (and this remains true) that opposition to the Assembly's departure from adherence to Scripture comes from people who love the Church of Scotland.

2. Of course the Bible teaches that homosexual people are to be loved and valued. It has been easy for liberals/revisionists to paint a negative picture of so-called 'homophobes' who have a personal animosity to homosexual people. This is wrong. 'The whole law is fulfilled in one word: "You shall love your neighbour as yourself"' (Gal. 5:14).

3. I sought to answer the charge that conservatives were in effect denying a congregation the hard-won right to call the minister of their choice. That was not the issue at stake. The issue was: who may legitimately and scripturally *be* a Church of Scotland minister.

4. I responded to the allegation that evangelicals are schismatics who want to divide the Church. Again this allegation is

[1] The Assembly had sought to impose a 'moratorium' on any public pronouncements on the subject. The journalist, Kenneth Roy, in the online *Scottish Review* (28 May 2009) described an e-mail he had received from a Church of Scotland minister who wrote, 'I would dearly love to respond to your atheistic commentator, but we are now being gagged by a "moratorium".' Roy says that he contacted the Acting Principal Clerk of Assembly, but could not report her reply: 'I am unable to tell you what was in it since her e-mail was headed, "Not for Publication". Is this really a sensible way for the Church of Scotland to conduct its business through the crisis it faces?'

simply not true. Our great desire is for the Church to be united on the basis of the Bible as its supreme rule of faith and life. The concern in 2009 was that the Church of Scotland, by its decision in General Assembly, had forced a division by permitting what Scripture forbids. We believe that it is the liberals who are the real schismatics, in that they depart from the faith once for all delivered to God's people (Jude 3). They are the ones who are divisive.

This last point was recognised in an earlier time by Harvard New Testament scholar Kirsopp Lake (1872–1946) who opposed so-called 'Fundamentalism' in the controversies that enveloped the American church in the early part of the twentieth century, yet wrote with striking candour:

> It is a mistake, often made by educated men who happen to have but little knowledge of historical theology, to suppose that Fundamentalism is a new and strange form of thought. It is nothing of the kind; it is ... a theology that was once universally held by all Christians. How many were there, for instance, in the Christian Churches, in the eighteenth century, who doubted the infallible inspiration of all Scripture? A few, perhaps, but very few. No, the Fundamentalist may be wrong; I think he is. But it is we who have departed from the tradition, not he, and I am sorry for anyone who tries to argue with a Fundamentalist on the basis of authority. The Bible, and the *corpus theologicum* of the Church, is (*sic*) on the Fundamentalist side.[1]

2011

The 2009 Assembly also set up a Special Commission of nine persons, 'representative of the breadth and unity of the Church, to consult with all Presbyteries and Kirk Sessions and to prepare a study on Ordination and Induction to the Ministry of the Church of Scotland in the light of the issues addressed in a Report

[1] *The Religion of Yesterday and Tomorrow* (London, 1925), 61-62 – quoted by Nigel Cameron in *Pulpit and People* (Rutherford House, Edinburgh, 1986), 30.

welcomed by the General Assembly of 2007: "A challenge to unity: same-sex relationships as an issue in theology and human sexuality", and in light of the issues raised by the appeal against Aberdeen Presbytery's decision.'

The Special Commission prepared a consultation paper inviting Presbyteries and Kirk Sessions to express their views on questions arising from the Commission's remit and the divisions in the Church which led to its appointment. The Commission also prepared a DVD in which two ministers would present the conservative and revisionist positions. Every Presbytery and Kirk Session was to hold a special meeting on this subject, and evangelical people sought to express the so-called traditionalist view, even though many felt that the horse had already bolted from the stable in 2009 and that the Commission had then been given the remit of considering whether stable doors were best left open or kept shut.

Many people commented on the strange logic of approving the induction of a practising homosexual (as the 2009 Assembly had done) and at the same time saying, 'Maybe that isn't right, so let's look at it.' Is it not obvious that matters of principle need to be addressed before particular cases are considered and that the particular cases ought to be considered in light of the principles?

On Monday 23 May 2011 the Special Commission presented its report and placed before the Assembly a choice between two opposing 'trajectories'. The Commission reported, on the basis of the responses from Presbyteries and Kirk Sessions, that there was no impetus for change. During the debate, it was argued cogently and clearly that any proposals to allow the induction and ordination of practising homosexuals:

- would be counter to the will of the clear majority of elders and ministers in the Church
- would split the Church of Scotland
- would separate the Church of Scotland from the worldwide church of all the centuries and destroy ecumenical relations

• and, most seriously, would represent a rejection of the word of God in Scripture as the Church's rule of faith and life.

Despite excellent speeches by so-called 'traditionalists', who emphasised the crucial importance of these questions and pleaded with the Church to stand by its own title-deeds, the Assembly treated Scripture in a cavalier fashion and effectively rejected God's word; one speaker (an elder, who would probably never have imagined how often his words would subsequently be quoted) blatantly said that *we now know better than the Bible.*[1] This is in stark contrast with the testimony of a homosexual in a Report to the General Assembly of 1995 who wrote:

> We have taken to heart the truth of God's word in passages such as 1 Corinthians 6:9-10 and 1 Timothy 1:10 in its prohibition of active homosexual encounters of all kinds. As Christian believers, we honestly seek to interpret our predilection in the light of Scripture rather than interpret Scripture in the light of our predilection.[2]

The 2011 Assembly set the Church's trajectory towards the acceptance of practising homosexuals and also set up a Theological Commission which was in effect told which direction it should take – not so much *whether* but *how* to move forward to the revisionist position. The Commission was also given the task of preparing liturgies for the blessing of civil partnerships!

The effect of that day's business was that many ministers, elders and members of the Church of Scotland felt ashamed, dismayed, and angered. They were not left in any doubt about the direction the Church of Scotland was taking, despite the efforts of some officials to downplay it; the Moderator of the Assembly said in a

[1] Cf. Warfield's assertion that in rejecting external authority we have but naïvely assumed infallibility for ourselves! F. G. Zaspel, *The Theology of B. B. Warfield* (IVP, 2010), 51. Iain H. Murray has written, 'authentic Christianity will not be long preserved where Scripture is not recognised as the watershed between truth and error. On one side of the watershed is submission to all that God has spoken; on the other side is the human wish to decide what is trustworthy and what is not.' *Evangelical Holiness and Other Addresses* (Banner of Truth, 2013), 64.

[2] Quoted in *Truth and Love in a Sexually Disordered World*, ed. Searle, 54.

press statement that he wanted to stress that *no decisions* had been made – although he went on in his next sentence to express the hope that those who disagreed *with what had been decided* would nevertheless remain part of the Church.

The debate was described as the most prayed-for debate in many years; as well as praying for a change of heart, people had prayed for a clear decision rather than the expected 'fudge'. The first request was not granted but the second was; the die was cast. Even so, evangelicals hoped and prayed that the Assembly of 2013 would reverse the decisions made in 2009 and 2011.

2013

In 2013 the Theological Commission presented its report and it was during the ensuing debate that a former Moderator came up with an unanticipated motion: he moved that the General Assembly should 'affirm the Church's historic and current doctrine and practice in relation to human sexuality; nonetheless permit those Kirk Sessions who wish to depart from that doctrine and practice to do so.'

The motion was so obviously self-contradictory that it surprised many of us that it was taken seriously, but it became clear that he really meant it, and some of us tried to persuade the Assembly of the absurdity and wrong-headedness of moving to such a bizarre decision.

It was pointed out that over the past few years, the Church of Scotland had already lost congregations, ministers, members, and money, while other individual members of congregations had been hanging on by the skin of their teeth, hoping against hope – and praying – that the Church would not only make up its mind once and for all on this issue, but would make up its mind to stand by that which it constantly professes to be its supreme rule of faith and life. The point was made that what was at stake was not a number of inductions but the question of whether the Church would stand by the teaching of Scripture – which the members of the Commission agreed[1] is clear on the issue of homosexual practice – or whether the Assembly would claim to know better than the God who, as the church down the centuries has believed, inspired the writing of the Scriptures. It was also argued that the adoption of the former Moderator's so-called compromise deliverance would amount to a betrayal of our Lord and a failure in leadership. It would also open the door to the kind of suggested order of service in the Report for the blessing of same-sex relationships – a document which many people would never in their worst nightmares have envisaged appearing in a Report to the Church of Scotland's General Assembly.[2]

Despite all pleas for the Assembly to reject the patently self-contradictory motion, the Assembly accepted it and confirmed the downward trajectory which had been followed year after year. As amendment after amendment was rejected by the Assembly, Bible-believers felt increasingly marginalised and frozen out.

It was claimed by many during and after the Assembly, with a strange kind of inverted logic, that the decision was (in the words of the then Principal Clerk) 'a massive vote for the peace and unity of the Church', a compromise decision that should cater for both sides of the argument. In truth, it was no compromise at all but a complete surrender to the liberal position, reminiscent of the story of the couple doing interior decorating where she wanted green and he wanted blue, so they compromised and went for green!

The illogicality was recognised by a newspaper columnist who referred to the

[1] Cf. 'Report of Theological Commission on Same-sex Relationships and the Ministry' in *Reports to 2013 General Assembly*, page 20/65: 'every single reference to homosexual acts in the entire Bible is negative and condemnatory, as everyone on the Theological Commission recognises'.

[2] It included a prayer of thanks for 'your guidance in the lives of N... and N... (*i.e.*, John & Jim or Mary & Wendy), for the joy they have found in each other, and for the love and trust they bring to the happiness of this day'; the vow would be: 'In the presence of God, and before these witnesses, I, N..., affirm my love for you, N..., and my commitment to our partnership. I promise to love and respect you, to be faithful and loyal to you, for as long as we live'; and the minister would then say, 'N... and N..., may God's richest blessing be upon you both. May God give you joy in your life together.'

> so-called compromise measure which, if anything, aggravated the divisions in the church. It insisted that it was maintaining the Kirk's historic teaching on sexual matters but agreed to allow individual congregations or kirk sessions to call a homosexual minister who was in a civil partnership if they wished. The contradictory character of that ruling was more reminiscent of politicians' conduct than of a religious denomination affirming Christian teaching. ... What has disgusted the public with politicians is their weasel words; they expect better from churches.[1]

Writing after the 2013 Assembly,[2] the Rev. Andrew Randall, now minister of Grace Church, Larbert (a congregation of the International Presbyterian Church), described the decision of the Assembly as:

- misguided in its aims – setting aside truth in the interests of a false unity
- dishonest in its effects – claiming to stand for one thing, while implementing the opposite
- and disastrous in its outcome – propelling the church further down a path of liberalisation which will be its destruction.

He stressed what needs constant stressing:

> This is not a debate about the value or dignity of individuals. To accept what God says about same-sex relationships is neither homophobic nor unloving, both of which would be entirely wrong. Our great desire is that *all* men and women, whatever their circumstances, might come to know the joy of God's gracious salvation. However, the way in which we come to receive the benefits of the gospel is by repentance and faith.
>
> - *Repentance* means turning from all known sin. We can only do this if we allow God to tell us what behaviours are sinful.

[1] Gerald Warner, 'Saturday Essay', *Daily Mail*, 15 June 2013.

[2] In a paper circulated within Larbert Old Parish Church (where he then ministered) on 23 June 2013. It dealt with the two questions: 'Why we consider the decision of the 2013 General Assembly unacceptable', and 'Why we have decided to leave the Church of Scotland.'

> • *Faith* means believing what God has said, trusting what He has promised, and doing what He has commanded.
>
> This means that it is not possible to claim Jesus as Saviour and Lord while continuing in an unrepentantly sinful lifestyle. Jesus' call to discipleship is a call to obedience in every area of life, including our sexuality – whether we are married or single, heterosexual or homosexual. To affirm as right what God has called wrong is to entrench men and women in unrepentant sinful behaviour, and so place them in grave spiritual peril. In addition, any church which rejects God's word forfeits the right to expect God's blessing. The church lives or dies by its faithfulness to the Scriptures, and we believe that the decision of 20 May 2013 will do untold spiritual harm throughout the land for many years to come.

2014

When the Legal Questions Committee presented its report to the 2014 General Assembly, a counter-motion was presented in the hope of turning the Assembly back from its previous rejection of biblical teaching; it asked the Assembly to 'Affirm the Church's historic and current position that, according to God's revealed will in Scripture, marriage between one man and one woman is the only right and proper context for sexual relations.' This counter-motion also sought to re-affirm the duty of the Church to minister to all people, regardless of their sexual orientation, recognising in particular the burden felt by those who struggle with same-sex attraction while striving to maintain a celibate life, and that same-sex attraction is not, in itself, a barrier to leadership in the Church.

The counter-motion was ably presented by the Rev. Jeremy Middleton who referred to the Scripture reading at the beginning of the Assembly:

> The Scripture reading was Hosea 11:1-9 – a powerful, challenging, plea-laden rebuke to a people who had stubbornly refused to heed his word: and a word now spoken into the leadership

> body of a Church, which for the past three years has consistently been warned that to adopt any other line on this matter is to depart from the clear and consistent teaching of the Scriptures. '*My people are determined to turn from me: though they call me God Most High, I will not exalt them.*' Could there have been a clearer warning given by the Lord through his word about the import of such a determination to turn away from his plain instruction in Scripture? And yet, in the face of that the General Assembly chose, by a substantial majority, not to vote for a clear re-statement of the scriptural position.

After debate the counter-motion was defeated by 369 votes to 189.

2015

The 2015 General Assembly received the report on Presbyteries' responses to the Overture which had been sent to them under the Barrier Act. Fourteen Presbyteries had voted against the so-called compromise position but 31 voted in favour, and it was for the 2015 Assembly either to convert the Overture into Church law or depart from the matter.

On Saturday 16 May the Overture was approved by 309 votes to 182. This authorises congregations to depart from 'the Church's historic and current position' and call a minister in a same-sex civil partnership.

The following Thursday, the Assembly received a joint report from its Theological Forum and Legal Questions Committee on the question of whether this authorisation should be extended to ministers in same-sex 'marriages'. It was decided by 213 votes to 205 to approve of such an extension, although it was then moved and agreed (215 votes to 195) that the matter should be sent down to Presbyteries for their consideration. The decision to allow congregations to call a minister in a same-sex 'marriage' was effectively approved subject to the agreement of the majority of Presbyteries and the following General Assembly.[1]

[1] It might be added that in June 2015 the Kirk Session of at least one congregation

Following this approval in principle, many members and friends of the Church of Scotland have in various ways expressed their dismay at the direction in which the Church has moved. For example, a widely-reported Pastoral Statement from the Presbytery of Lewis spoke of the Presbytery's desire to

> distance ourselves from the decisions that have been made. We believe that these decisions represent a denial of and departure from the clear teaching of God's word that such relationships are to be between one man and one woman, and that always within the context of marriage.[1]

Another outcome has been that the General Assembly of the Presbyterian Church of Ireland decided to decline the invitation to be represented at the 2016 Assembly of the Church of Scotland. The Russian Orthodox Church had cut off ecumenical relationships with the Church of Scotland over this issue, and the Moderator of the Australian Presbyterian Church, David Cook, who attended the 2015 Church of Scotland Assembly, wrote,

> Just as the Reformation was about more than the indulgence issue, so the malaise of the Church of Scotland is wider and deeper than this one issue. The majority has rejected the authority of God himself in admitting to Christian ministry those living in such relationships. I recognise that faithful congregations have left the Church of Scotland and that others have remained and opposed such abuse of the word of God, but I see no point in symbolically representing the Presbyterian Church of Australia at such an Assembly, when the basis of our fellowship, the Lordship of the risen Lord Jesus Christ, is so disregarded. Our mother Church has tragically left the family home.[2]

---

has gone through the process agreed by the General Assembly and decided that it is open to having a minister who is living in a civil partnership.

[1] Responding to this Statement, the acting Clerk of Assembly, claimed, 'What is important in the statement from the Presbytery of Lewis is the expressed commitment to participate fully in the life of the Church of Scotland despite their obvious disappointment at the General Assembly decision.'

[2] http://www.presbyterian.org.au/index.php/resources/moderator-s-comments/8-the-church-of-scotland (posted 21 May 2015; accessed 4 July 2015).

3

To Leave or Not To Leave

THE decisions of recent General Assemblies have placed Church of Scotland evangelicals in an extremely difficult position. Should they swallow hard and get on with the task of ministering in their parishes – 'you in your small corner and I in mine'? Should they resign? Should they seek to lead their congregations to secede from the denomination? Should they seek to form some kind of conservative Church within a Church?

In the aftermath of each decision of the Assembly, there have been statements from the 'establishment' to the effect that there is no crisis in the Church of Scotland, and when individuals have taken decisive action statements have been forthcoming regarding the smallness and insignificance of the steps taken. A similar thing happened in the period of the Disruption in 1843,[1] and it has been insisted in recent times by moderators, clerks and others that present controversies are but a tiny evangelical storm in a large ecclesiastical tea-cup. The plainly self-contradictory notion that the church should simultaneously hold to its traditional position while allowing those who wish to depart from it to do so has been hailed as something that supposedly serves the peace and unity of the Church!

In one of his books Alister McGrath has suggested that, prior to the disagreements brought into the open after the famous interchange between John Stott and Martyn Lloyd-Jones in 1966, the

[1] On 17 May 1843 the *Scotsman* said, 'There will be no disruption in the church.'

issue of separation from mixed denominations 'had been an issue of friendly disagreement among evangelicals, but had not been seen as a "gospel issue"'.[1] There have always been many issues of 'friendly disagreement' among evangelicals, whether large matters such as baptismal practice or smaller ones such as whether to sit, stand or kneel for public prayer. But when does a dispute become a gospel issue?

Our belief is that the present crisis has become a gospel issue (a) because it affects the issue of salvation and (b) because the Church's adherence to Scripture is foundational to its existence.

In relation to the first of these issues, the Bible *does* present the matter as a gospel issue. It says: 'Do not be deceived: neither the sexually immoral, nor idolaters, nor adulterers, nor men who practise homosexuality, nor thieves, nor the greedy, nor drunkards, nor revilers, nor swindlers will inherit the kingdom of God' (1 Cor. 6:9-10). It is expressed as plainly as that. 'Traditionalists' are sometimes challenged about the fact that greed is mentioned alongside homosexual practice (in the same way as Gal. 5:19-21 lists jealousy, rivalries and envy as 'works of the flesh' alongside sexual immorality and other sins). This is a challenge we must take seriously; there is no graded list of sins in order of seriousness. All Christians need God's forgiveness and the Spirit's power to be continually transformed so that we may 'grow in the grace and knowledge of our Lord and Saviour Jesus Christ' (2 Pet. 3:18).

At one stage in the course of the recent controversies a minister wrote to me about a question which he had asked in the General Assembly. The question was: 'Since we live not under law but within the realm of grace, do you believe that it is possible for a couple living in a same-sex partnership, who are a source of blessing to one another and to those among whom they live, to be justified by faith in Jesus Christ?'

Clearly I was supposed to answer in the affirmative, but I wondered: what would my questioner have said if the question were

[1] A. McGrath, *To Know and Serve God* (Hodder & Stoughton, 1997), 121.

returned to him with the following amendment: 'Since we live not under law but within the realm of grace, do you believe that it is possible for a serial adulterer or bank-robber to be justified by faith in Jesus Christ?'

The invitation of the gospel is to all who will respond to the message of God's grace (*e.g.*, Rev. 22:17), but what does that response involve? God's call is for repentance. In the case of stealing, for example, 'Let the thief no longer steal' (Eph. 4:28), and when the question is asked in relation to people who practise homosexuality, repentance would mean a change of behaviour.

As for the second issue – adherence to Scripture as foundational for the church: not all evangelicals have taken the line that departure is called for.[1] Not only are evangelicals increasingly divided from liberals, but within evangelicalism there has opened up a breach that threatens fellowship.

The liberal establishment has tried to keep the lid on 'rebellion', denying that there is any crisis, and at the same time making life difficult for those who have resolved to secede rather than swallow the compromise, mixed-economy decision of the General Assembly. As the land-owners at the time of the Disruption did all in their power to obstruct the growth of the Free Church, so in recent times the liberal and legal establishment within the Church of Scotland has sought to put obstacles in the way of seceders.

There have been some exceptions. In a few cases, members of presbyteries have been less hostile and in some cases have tried to work co-operatively with those who have reluctantly decided to leave. Some ministers, for example, have been given permission to remain in their manses while seeking guidance about the future, but in most cases leavers have met with little sympathy and much opposition. Yet the seceding ministers have done nothing wrong;

[1] Even at the time of the Disruption they did not. Shortly after that major event, James McCosh, a Free Church minister and editor of *The Dundee Warder*, calculated that of the 741 ministers who remained in the Church of Scotland about a third were evangelicals (260) while the remaining two-thirds were 'of the old Moderate type'. J. Wolffe, *The Expansion of Evangelicalism* (IVP, 2006), 220-21.

they have not acted illegally or immorally. In fact, for all their personal imperfections, their aim has been to stand for what the Church of Scotland has always stood for and to remain faithful to the Church's own standards.

But when we come to the question of evangelical responses to the crisis, there has arisen a surprising degree of difference. Around the time of the 2009 decision to allow Aberdeen Presbytery to induct a practising homosexual to a charge, it was hoped by some that there would be a concerted evangelical response, even if it would not have resembled the strength and scope of the Disruption of 1843. A number of meetings, large and small, were held; different evangelical groupings were formed, and in the process of writing this book I have seen many papers written by evangelicals who have been wrestling with the question of how to counter what they all regard as the denomination's rejection of Scripture.

Such considerations give the lie to the charge that some people have simply run away at the first sign of trouble or taken an easy way out to soothe their conscience! The truth is that evangelicals have tried for a long time to influence an increasingly liberal denomination. Departure from the Church of Scotland has certainly not been an 'easy way out'. For many evangelicals such decisions have been very costly (as we will see further towards the end of this chapter).

What to Do?

With regard to the specifics of what action should be taken in the wake of the decisions of recent Assemblies, various possible responses have been considered. These have included:

- initiating some kind of 'Associate Presbytery' or 'Relief Church' within the Church of Scotland

- joining an existing Presbyterian denomination, such as the Free Church of Scotland or the International Presbyterian Church

- forming a new denomination

• going the way of independency, with or without affiliation to a body such as the Fellowship of Independent Evangelical Churches.

In addition there was a suggestion that dissenting congregations should remain within the Church of Scotland but follow a policy of non-cooperation with the denomination's central structures. This might have involved the withholding of payments to central funds, opting out of united services, objecting to the appointment of any practising homosexual to lead a visitation to a congregation, non-attendance at Presbytery, *etc.* In some places members were withholding their offerings and trust funds were set up, giving people the choice of whether to contribute to the central funds of the Church or to allocate their offerings differently. However, this policy of disengagement did not commend itself to many. Apart from the obvious inter-personal difficulties that would arise, many felt that some of these actions would involve a failure to be true to their own vow to take their due part in the life of the Church, and that so long as they were still part of the Church of Scotland they ought to fulfil their responsibility as members.

But that responsibility is not an unqualified one. One of the questions put to ministers is 'Do you promise to be subject in the Lord to this Presbytery and to the superior courts of the Church?' The normal response is, 'I do', but I heard one ordinand respond more fully: 'In the Lord, I do' – making the point that the context of submission to the Church is a prior commitment and submission to the Lord. When a clash arises between submission to the denomination and submission to the Lord, the priority lies with submission to the Lord (Acts 5:29).

Another promise required of ministers is 'to seek the peace and unity of this Church'. Such a promise underlines the seriousness of secession, but the belief of those who have sadly departed from the denomination is that it is liberalism that has violated the Church's internal peace. This means that the way to be true to vows which were, after all, made to God (not merely to a denomination) is to adhere to our first commitment to him.

One of the efforts to bring conservative people together (as has already been mentioned) was the formation of the Fellowship of Confessing Churches (established in April 2009). Several meetings were held and congregations were invited to sign up, by resolution of their Kirk Session, as members of FCC. Sixty-five congregations did so, but once it became clear that nearly all of the members of the organising committee were committed to leaving the Church of Scotland it was felt by the committee members that it would be better to close FCC down (31 December 2011) rather than leave a residual but leaderless organisation that was unlikely to organise anything.

One of the possibilities considered within FCC and elsewhere was the development of something similar to the Relief Church of the eighteenth century. This was a denomination (although at first it was not a denomination but a presbytery remaining within the Church of Scotland) formed in 1761 under Thomas Gillespie. It provided a place of relief for ministers and congregations who objected to patronage and the imposition of ministers on congregations. Some had hoped that such a solution might have been found, with the purpose of providing mutual support and fellowship, giving public expression to a rejection of the course which the Church was taking, and giving some solidarity for the future rather than leaving individual ministers, Kirk Sessions and members to their own devices.

Another suggestion was the formation of some kind of new structure as an attempt to bring together the various branches of Scottish Presbyterianism that hold a high view of Scripture. Whether such a plan could have attracted wide support is a huge question and there would have been the possibility that it would simply create yet another denomination, one that would operate alongside 'continuing' groups from those already in existence.

However, none of the endeavours to encourage a united response bore any fruit, and individual evangelical ministers and members have had to think, pray, and act on their own initiative.

Within the evangelical constituency there has been a surprisingly strong lobby of stayers. Some have said that they will remain within the Church of Scotland no-matter-what, and claimed historical support by referring to the ongoing influence of notable evangelical leaders such as the late William Still, minister of Gilcomston South Church, Aberdeen from 1945 to 1997. It is well-known that Mr Still, a forthright evangelical, advocated a policy of quiet infiltration – that is, for evangelicals to work and witness within congregations in such a way as to bring the denomination as a whole back to its evangelical roots.

It may be said incidentally that the Church of Scotland probably does not realise how much it owes to Mr Still. Such was his influence and charisma that, if he had acted in earlier days to lead an evangelical exodus from the Church of Scotland, the division might have been much greater.

Some people have claimed that Mr Still would never have left the Church of Scotland. In one of his books he wrote:

> Like Jesus and Paul and all the Old Testament prophets we must never, until the last desperate agonising moment, perpetrate schism, and take ourselves out of a nominal or backsliding Church. ... I believe no-one need leave the Kirk as long as its foundations remain, however far the generality have departed from it.[1]

The big question, of course, is whether we have reached 'the last desperate agonising moment' and whether the Kirk's 'foundations remain'.

Similarly James Philip, minister in Gardenstown from 1949 to 1958 and of Holyrood Abbey Church, Edinburgh from 1958 to 1997, another notable evangelical who had a large influence on many people in the Church of Scotland (ministers and members), believed in working steadily, persistently, and prayerfully for change within the denomination – change that would repudiate liberalism and bring the Church back to its foundations.

[1] *The Work of the Pastor* (1984; Paternoster & Rutherford House, 1996), 123-24.

In May 1969 Mr Philip, in his letter in the congregation's magazine, *The Record*, posed the question: 'What are we to say of the determination, expressed by a considerable number of evangelicals throughout the country to withdraw – and get all other evangelicals to withdraw with them – from the organised denominations because of their involvement and complicity with the ecumenical movement and its Romeward trend?'

Two years later (in the June 1971 *Record*) he referred to the life and ministry of Samuel, and of how

> God had finally to bypass the established order to bring about spiritual renewal in the land. He could not wait indefinitely for a change of heart in those he had called to serve him in his work, and so finally Eli, and all he stood for, was set aside, and a new leadership was given. Eli stands for the establishment in this story; and it was the establishment that God set aside in these days, in order to do a new thing in Israel.'

There followed this interesting comment in his reflections on the General Assembly of that year (1971):

> The time may be running out for the establishment to give a moral and spiritual lead to the nation, as was urged by the Lord High Commissioner on the opening day of the Assembly. We have often thought – and said – that it would be wonderful if a clear word from God were to ring out from the General Assembly for our troubled and anxious time. But what if that word is not to be spoken, what if it is no longer capable of being spoken by the established Church? Is it not just possible that God will speak in other ways, and through other channels? One thing at least is clear: time is not on the Church's side, and it will take more than the radical re-structuring of ecclesiastical framework to recover the ground that has been lost and prevent 'Ichabod'[1] being written over our page of the Church's history.

[1] Name given to her son by a daughter-in-law of Eli. It means 'Where is the glory?' 1 Samuel 4:21: 'She named the child Ichabod, saying, "The glory has departed from Israel ... for the ark of God has been captured."'

Would he have advocated departure from the denomination now? Some have claimed his support for a policy of 'staying in' no-matter-what, but his son William[1] recalls that just before his own induction to St George's Tron, Glasgow in 2004, his father said to him that the time would almost certainly come in William's ministry when true evangelicals would be so at odds with the establishment that they would be pushed out. This was five years before Mr Philip died but he was still able then to discuss such things, and his son has written, in relation to the secession of most of the Holyrood congregation to form the new Holyrood Evangelical Church in Edinburgh, 'I am in no doubt that were he living my father would have supported what Holyrood has done.'

James Philip's widow, Mary, says that she has often been asked, 'What would Jim have done?' She speaks about Jim's loyalty to the denomination and how he spoke of remaining in it unless and until he was 'put out', but she adds:

> I do think though that he would have felt that its current departure from the Scriptures, and *official* support of Kirk Sessions and congregations if they wish to appoint a minister living in an active homosexual relationship *would* amount to 'putting him out' of the established Church. People have pointed out to me that there have been far more serious departures from the Scriptures in ministers denying the uniqueness of Christ as the only way to God, the virgin birth and even the bodily resurrection of Christ, but although these men have not been disciplined – as far as I know – the church has never *officially* condoned this or indicated that such departure from Scripture was acceptable.

Her final comment was one of honest gratitude that he has been spared 'the desolation of seeing the downward spiral in the Church of Scotland and its departure from the historic faith'.

Such issues as the ordination of practising homosexuals to the ministry would probably never have entered the consciousness of Mr Still or Mr Philip, any more than a proposal to formulate an

[1] In an e-mail to the author, 31 October 2014.

evangelistic strategy for future missions to Mars! But it is interesting that, as far back as 1983, William Still, in a personal letter to Professor Sinclair B. Ferguson, expressed the view that the policy of quiet infiltration would not go on forever.[1]

Reasons for Staying

The present situation has given rise to a division within evangelicalism over the question of whether to leave or to stay.

The 'Perth Statement' of the Church of Scotland Evangelical Network (COSEN) refers to 'the current crisis over the ordination and induction of those in same-sex civil partnerships. Some have left the Kirk and others are considering doing so.' It then refers to its own formation as

> a network of evangelicals who have made the clear decision to remain in the Church of Scotland and to work for its reformation and renewal. We believe that the Church of Scotland remains an important vehicle for reaching the whole population of Scotland with the Gospel and, despite recent decisions, believe that God is still at work among us. We also believe that we can remain with integrity. We urge others to join with us and to remain in the Church of Scotland, as we seek to restore and rebuild our Church.[2]

In December 2014 another group was launched – the Covenant Fellowship – as a group within the Church of Scotland that would resist departure from the denomination and work for reform. It was launched in the wake of the revelation that a majority of Presbyteries had backed the overture that would allow

[1] It is of interest to consider what Mr Still meant by 'quiet infiltration'. It is often taken to mean a policy of seeking to gain power and influence in the committees and courts of the Church and thereby seeking to effect change in the denomination, whereas 'WS' was more concerned with seeking to increase the number of evangelical pulpits and congregations. The word 'infiltrate' is perhaps unfortunate since it seems to suggest altering the character of the denomination rather than bringing it back to its true and proper foundations as a scriptural and confessional church. It was liberalism that had infiltrated the denomination. In a phrase of James Packer's, it is liberalism that has 'only at best squatter's rights', *Honouring the People of God* (Paternoster, 1999), 334.

[2] 14 June 2013.

congregations to call practising homosexual people as ministers. Launching the new Fellowship, the Rev. Andrew McGowan said,

> The hope is that the Covenant Fellowship, which begins today as a protest against recent events, will grow to become an effective campaign group within the Church on behalf of those who believe in Christian orthodoxy.[1]

Such 'stay-ers' maintain that a decision to remain within the Church of Scotland does not equate with an acceptance of the decisions of the General Assembly. Actually it does! That is what is meant by Presbyterianism. They may register dissent but the decisions of the General Assembly are binding on the Church and while 'liberty of opinion' can be recognised in certain matters, the truth is that Assembly decisions define the position of the denomination. Those who remain in the denomination simply *are* part of it.

It has been argued that evangelicals who leave the Church thereby dilute evangelical influence in Presbyteries and Assemblies and make it so much harder to bring them back to a scriptural position. There is obvious force in this argument, but the whole point is that people who have left have done so precisely because they believe they would be disobedient to Scripture if they remained.

While there are those who have concluded that the Church of Scotland has passed a point of no return, some who advocate remaining within the denomination respond by saying that surely nothing is impossible for God, that the Lord is almighty and can make even the Valley of Achor, the place of defeat, into a door of hope (Hos. 2:15); they point to Genesis 18:14 and ask, 'Is anything too hard for the Lord?' Our response to that is to say that we must act, not on the basis of what God *can* do, but on the basis of what he *has* revealed in Scripture.

Another reason for staying in the Church of Scotland is the conviction that evangelicals are the *real* Church of Scotland. Why,

[1] http://www.heraldscotland.com/news/home-news/church-ministers-to-sign-covenant-against-gay-ordination.114826575 (accessed 29.12.14).

such evangelicals ask, should *we* leave? Should it not be the liberals who must leave the denomination? However, the Church of Scotland has taken an anti-scriptural stance year after year in her General Assemblies, and there surely comes a time for evangelicals to make a sad departure.

Some people take a parochial view that so long as 'the establishment' leave them alone to exercise a biblical, pastoral, and evangelical ministry in their parishes, there is no need to leave, and they can remain untainted by Assembly decisions. This argument has force, and indeed part of the tragedy of the denomination's liberal stance is the failure in Christian witness to the nation. But a pastor's calling is to care for his people and if the best way of caring for them is to lead them away from a liberal denomination, then that becomes his duty. Leaders are called to lead, after all, and good leadership will provide the best environment for nurturing believers and reaching out with the gospel into the community. Is it really an evidence of Christian compassion to remain in apparent fellowship with those who act against God's revealed will? One simply cannot remain part of a denomination and yet not be complicit in its decisions. The Church of Scotland, through its General Assembly, has decided to reject God's word and it is not valid for ministers or others to claim that they are not part of that position. The truth is that, so long as they remain within the denomination, they *are* part of it.

Other stayers point to the parable of the wheat and the tares (Matt. 13:24-30) and Jesus' teaching about allowing both to grow together until harvest time. If the parable referred to the *church*, then the words of the Confession of Faith would be relevant: 'The purest churches under heaven are subject both to mixture and error.'[1] However the parable begins, 'The kingdom of heaven may be compared to ...' (verse 24), and when the disciples asked Jesus to explain the parable, he specifically said, 'The field is the *world*' (Matt. 13:38). Verse 24 does not say that the kingdom may be

[1] Chapter XXV.5.

compared to the field but to the 'man who sowed good seed in his field'. It is a parable about differing responses to the message of the kingdom, and it is in the world that the wheat and tares grow together – until the harvest at the end of the age (verse 30).[1] Granted, the visible church may often be a mixed company, but this parable cannot be used to suggest that it is wrong to leave an unfaithful denomination.

So far as the church is concerned, we have:

• Paul's admonition not to receive a 'different gospel – not that there is another one, but there are some who trouble you and want to distort the gospel of Christ' (Gal. 1:6-7)

• John's word about 'testing the spirits' (1 John 4:1)

• and Jude's word about contending for 'the faith that was once for all delivered to the saints' (Jude 3). There is a givenness about Christianity which means that it is not open to redefinition or amendment. Methods in organisation and strategy may change and adapt but the message is *the message as given once and for all in Scripture.*

Other questions which face evangelicals who remain in an increasingly liberal denomination such as the Church of Scotland are:

1. If you stay in, doesn't that mean that the liberal denomination has you where it wants you – protesting and making a noise but nevertheless submitting to its liberal decisions after all? The Covenant Fellowship's statement says:

> We believe that the Church of Scotland is moving away from its roots in Scripture and the Westminster Confession of Faith. This Covenant Fellowship will draw together those who believe that the Scriptures, in their entirety, are the Word of God and must provide the basis for everything we believe and do. Our vision is nothing less than the reformation and renewal of the Church

[1] Cf. note on Matthew 13:30 in *ESV Student Study Bible*, p. 1264: 'Believers and unbelievers live side by side in the world until the day of judgment.'

of Scotland, in accordance with the Word of God and by the empowering of his life-giving Spirit.

The statement speaks strongly about the wrongness of the Church's present course, but it is telling that the (then) Acting Principal Clerk of the General Assembly, in a statement on the Church of Scotland's website, has welcomed the formation of the Covenant Fellowship and 'Professor McGowan's continued commitment to remain within the Church', though 'we disagree with his criticisms'.[1] If you intimate in advance that, whatever the denomination decides, you will stay in it, does that not amount to giving *carte blanche* to proceed further and further with their liberal agenda? The question may even be posed: Is there *anything* that the denomination might do that would merit an evangelical departure?

2. If people ask whether any good can come of secession (especially in light of repeated secessions over the centuries), we would insist that Christian people are called by God to do what is right, without having cast-iron guarantees about the future. They must trust God with the consequences of their actions undertaken in obedience to his commands. It may be sad that further division has been caused – hence the title of this book – but our first responsibility is to be faithful to God and his word.

3. Is it right that, after a minister leaves a congregation, the Kirk Session has to decide whether to take a revisionist or traditionalist line (that is, whether or not they are open to having a practising homosexual as their minister)? Far from fostering the unity of the church, this policy is a recipe for division and controversy. Few Kirk Sessions would be unanimous in their views on this matter, so a vote would have to be taken, which would itself be divisive; and would the disaffected minority be expected to simply roll over and accept the decision of the majority? In

[1] http://www.churchofscotland.org.uk/news_and_events/news/2014/statement-on-formation-of-gay-ordination-protest-group (accessed 29.12.14).

particular, are Bible-believing people – who believe that such a decision involves giving approval to something which is sinful in God's eyes – expected to go on as if nothing has happened?

4. What will happen when 'traditionalists' are targeted? The General Assembly was assured (20 May 2013), in answer to a question, that the denomination would support and indemnify any minister or elder against whom legal action was taken on account of his beliefs about the wrongness of same-sex relationships; but that does not address the emotional and personal costs; nor does it face the possibility that it will, at some future time, be the Church itself that will be putting pressure on people (as happened with the originally permissive legislation to allow the ordination of women).

5. Is not the present situation – the Church's acceptance of the legitimacy of same-sex relationships – cruel to people who experience same-sex attraction but seek to live a celibate life pleasing to God? One pastor has written on behalf of people who experience same-sex attraction but

> want to remain faithful to the teaching of the Bible. We do this, not only because we believe that God's word is good, but also because, in the end, we believe it signposts the route to human flourishing – and to life itself.[1]

Another has referred to the action of the Evangelical Alliance in terminating the membership of an affiliated organisation because of its acceptance of homosexual behaviour as 'a very painful decision to arrive at ... But for those of us battling same-sex attraction such decisions on the part of the Alliance are a huge encouragement.' Conversely, it is discouraging to see any professing evangelicals suggesting that this is an area of legitimate disagreement; this seems like 'telling us we needn't bother fighting on'.[2]

[1] Ed Shaw, http://www.eauk.org/church/stories/christians-and-same-sex-attraction-the-other-side-of-the-story.cfm (accessed 3.9.14).

[2] Sam Allberry in letter to editor: September/October 2014 issue of *IDEA* (magazine of Evangelical Alliance), 37.

A Costly Decision

The decision to leave the Church of Scotland has not been an easy one for ministers, elders or members of congregations. A leaflet produced by one new church (Holyrood Evangelical Church, Edinburgh) states, 'We seek to be faithful and obedient to the Bible, even when there is a cost.' For some it has indeed been costly to take a stand, and the willingness to face such costs is to be admired. The cost has been experienced in several ways:

• There has been an *emotional* cost. Some people have left congregations and buildings that have been part of their lives for many years and sometimes part of their family heritage. 'Leavers' have been of all ages. For example, in one of the new congregations there was a man in his nineties who made the principled decision to leave the congregation of which he had been a member all his life. While it is true, of course, that the church is not a building, and it is easy to say that Christian commitment does not depend on attachment to a building, yet the emotional cost of leaving such cherished places has been considerable for some.

• There has also been a *financial* cost. In some cases people have departed from buildings on which they had spent considerable amounts of their own money. Some have been faced with the cost of finding or perhaps eventually erecting new church buildings, as well as providing stipends and manses for their ministers. So far the outfall has not been on the scale of the post-Disruption era, but generous giving has been the response of many in the current crisis. I know of one new congregation that had an offering for the provision of a building and on two Sundays gathered £155,000; another has established a building fund and members have already pledged £420,000.

• There has been a *domestic* cost, especially for some ministers who have been placed in a situation of uncertainty. Faithfulness for them has involved facing up to such costs in very practical terms, some not being sure where they and their families will find accommodation. As noted above, the commitment of many members has been extraordinary in providing such help.

• For some there has been a *personal* cost in terms of stress and illness. The decisions of General Assemblies have caused much upset and many sleepless nights, and the stress of coping with uncertainty and pressure over a lengthy period has taken its toll on the health of some, including ministers and their families.

• There has also been a *relational* cost. Relationships have been strained since some congregations have experienced a parting of the ways. Those who have left and those who have stayed have sometimes found that the closeness of their former relationship has been strained. It is easy to say that it ought not to be so, but it simply has been a painful time for many people. This includes the divergence of view within the evangelical fraternity: there have been many assertions of a desire for continuing fellowship even when evangelicals go their different ways, but it cannot be denied that the turmoil of the times has put a strain on many relationships.

When the cost of departure is so high, why bother? Is it really worth taking such a costly step? To answer these questions we must next consider the teaching of Scripture, our supreme rule of faith and life, and understand the reasons why it is binding on God's church.

4

'Reach Me that Bible'

A long time ago, in an age when many people were unconvinced about the appropriateness of foreign missions, an evangelical minister called John Erskine (1721–1803) stood up in the General Assembly, pointed to the clerk's table and said, 'Moderator, rax me that Bible' (reach me that Bible). In his view, that was the great need; if there are differing views, reach for the Bible to settle the issue. Our contention in this book is that this is the Church's great need now – to reach for *the Book*.

In this chapter we take up the subject of what the Bible says about homosexual practice before coming in the next chapter to the 'So what?' question: Why should we believe in and act upon what is written in the Bible?

This ground has been traversed often in many books and papers, including the Report to the 2013 General Assembly of its Theological Commission on Same-Sex Relationships and the Ministry,[1] but a book such as this must include reference to what the Bible says on the subject. Without this foundation there is a real danger that the passage of time will lead many people into a weak, shoulder-shrugging acquiescence. The proposer of the compromise decision of the 2013 Assembly even expressed the hope that liberally-minded people would allow time for those who still have to catch up with them! The question has been posed what people's attitudes will be in twenty or thirty years' time from now, the

[1] *Reports to the General Assembly 2013*, section 20/3, especially pages 20/73-88.

implication being that the passage of time will bring acceptance of the changes rapidly taking place in our society. Part of the thrust of this book is to encourage people to resist the slow process of attrition that is at work and which insidiously attempts to wean them away from their adherence to God's truth – as if time can somehow change truth's absolute character.

In British society at large, the government probably expects that 'the people' will meekly come to accept their redefinition of marriage and the introduction of same-sex 'marriage' as a *fait accompli*; in the church, liberals probably anticipate a similar process of acquiescence. 'Conservatives', 'traditionalists', 'evangelicals' (whichever term is used) will be expected to moan and complain for a while but they will gradually come to accept the ordination of practising homosexuals.

What, then, does the Bible say about the particular matter that has caused the present crisis? We maintain that the issue of scriptural authority is the crux of the controversy. This is so because of the Bible's teaching on the particular issue of homosexual practice. It may not deal specifically with the subject of homosexual *orientation*, but if the Bible prohibits homosexual *practice*, then the challenge to faithfulness arises – as it does with everything else that the Bible teaches. Jesus himself said, 'Scripture cannot be broken' (John 10:35); William Lorimer expresses it in Scots, 'Scriptur is no tae set aside'[1] (not to be set aside).

The Words of Scripture

What then does the Bible say about homosexual practice? The main relevant passages are as follows:

• Genesis 1:27; 2:24: 'God created man in his own image, in the image of God he created him; male and female he created them. ... a man shall leave his father and his mother and hold fast to his wife, and they shall become one flesh.'

[1] William Lorimer, *The New Testament in Scots* (Southside Publishers, 1983), 180.

- Genesis 19:5, 24: 'The men of the city ... called to Lot, "Where are the men who came to you tonight? Bring them out to us, that we may know them." ... The LORD rained on Sodom and Gomorrah sulphur and fire from the LORD out of heaven.'

- Leviticus 18:22: 'You shall not lie with a male as with a woman; it is an abomination.'

- Matthew 19:4-5: 'Jesus answered, "Have you not read that he who made them from the beginning made them male and female and said, 'Therefore a man shall leave his father and his mother and hold fast to his wife, and the two shall become one flesh.'"'

- Romans 1:21-27: 'Although they knew God, they did not honour him as God or give thanks to him, but they became futile in their thinking, and their foolish hearts were darkened. Claiming to be wise, they became fools, and exchanged the glory of the immortal God for images resembling mortal man and birds and animals and creeping things. Therefore God gave them up to dishonourable passions. For their women exchanged natural relations for those that are contrary to nature; and the men likewise gave up natural relations with women and were consumed with passion for one another, men committing shameless acts with men.'

- 1 Corinthians 6:9-11: 'Do not be deceived: neither the sexually immoral, nor idolaters, nor adulterers, nor men who practise homosexuality, nor thieves, nor the greedy, nor drunkards, nor revilers, nor swindlers will inherit the kingdom of God. And such were some of you ...'

- 1 Timothy 1:9-11: '... the law is not laid down for the just but for the lawless and disobedient, for the ungodly and sinners, for the unholy and profane, for those who strike their fathers and mothers, for murderers, the sexually immoral, men who practise homosexuality, enslavers, liars, perjurers, and whatever else is contrary to sound doctrine, in accordance with the gospel of the glory of the blessed God.'

It is only special pleading that can evade the plain message of these passages.[1] The cumulative force of these passages makes it so abundantly plain that 'not only the learned, but the unlearned, in a due use of the ordinary means, may attain unto a sufficient understanding'.[2]

In the first chapter of his epistle to the Romans, Paul argues that same-sex sexual activity (he not only treats male and female acts as equivalent, but actually mentions women first) is 'contrary to nature' (Rom. 1:26). Common sense and elementary biology teach us that the male body and the female body naturally 'fit' – which is also clearly what the Bible says to all who look at the matter objectively.

A former chairman of Forward Together[3] quoted a professor from Murdoch University in Australia who supports the induction of homosexuals, but has written,

> In the current discussions about homosexuality, some issues should be clear from the start. One is that the Bible roundly condemns homosexuality and homosexual activity. *Of this there is not a shadow of a doubt.* Its writers deplored homosexual acts as a deliberate perversion of human nature, a flouting of God's intention in creation.

It is sometimes argued that the biblical case against homosexual practice rests on a few verses only and that references to homosexual behaviour in the Bible are rare. The late David F. Wright responded to such arguments by saying that such references are few and brief because homosexual acts were self-evidently wrong:

[1] Cf. Charles Hodge's remark in another context, 'It is an unnatural interpretation which no one would adopt except to suit a purpose.' *Systematic Theology*, vol. 3, 325-6.

[2] Westminster Confession of Faith, I.7.

[3] A conservative group within the Church of Scotland which seeks to support and encourage those of evangelical persuasion in their witness to Jesus Christ as Lord and Saviour and to present a biblical perspective on the life and work of the Church of Scotland in order to maintain its evangelical heritage, especially on issues of contemporary debate. See http://ftscotland.wordpress.com. Forward Together has now merged into Covenant Fellowship Scotland.

> There is no evidence whatsoever that Israel or primitive Christianity needed any debate to determine whether the homosexual phenomena they encountered were displeasing to God. If this issue was not a big one in the apostolic churches (or among the Old Testament people of God), this was not because they could not make up their minds about it, or thought that it did not really matter one way or the other. It was an open-and-shut case.[1]

Back in 2007 a 'Report to the General Assembly of the Church of Scotland on Human Sexuality' stated (section 4.13.18),

> Although the Group reflects different views on what the church's attitude to homosexuality should be, there was somewhat surprise at the degree of concord reached regarding the plain meaning of Scripture in the specific mentions of same-sex sexual activity. … There was almost a weariness with interested readings of certain key texts, which tortuously attempt to repudiate the writer's clear intention to condemn behaviour as bad. The Bible, when it occasionally takes up the subject of same-sex activity, presents it as a wrong choice.

Similarly the 'Report of the Theological Commission on Same-sex Relationships and the Ministry' could report to the 2013 Assembly that

> every single reference to homosexual acts in the entire Bible is negative and condemnatory, as everyone on the Theological Commission recognises.[2] … Everyone on the Theological Commission (on both sides of this debate) agrees that there is not one positive reference to homosexuality in the entire Bible. This agreement is significant.[3]

These quotations come from the section of the Report written by traditionalists but they are interesting in what they assert about the agreement of all on what the Bible says.

[1] David F. Wright, *The Christian Faith and Homosexuality* (Rutherford House, 1994), 8.

[2] *Reports to General Assembly 2013*, page 20/65, section 7.2.

[3] *Ibid.*, page 20/71, section 7.5 (b).

The Commission as a whole makes the candid assessment:

> For Traditionalists within the Church, issues of human sexuality, as presented in the current debate, have become a matter of critical theological concern. Equally, the debate is perceived to be one in which the very status of the Scriptures of the Old and New Testaments is threatened and their teaching undermined. From that perspective, if the Church as a whole were to depart from the teaching of Scripture, as understood by Traditionalists,[1] in relation to issues of human sexuality, it would thereby distance itself from the reality of what it means to be an integral part of the 'One Holy, Catholic and Apostolic Church', and the Church of Scotland could no longer affirm that it 'adheres to the Scottish Reformation; receives the Word of God which is contained in the Scriptures of the Old and New Testaments as its supreme rule of faith and life; and avows the fundamental doctrines of the Catholic faith founded thereupon.'[2]

'Contained In'

The above paragraph makes reference to the words 'contained in', a phrase which features in the statement (or preamble) read at ordination services in which the Church of Scotland 'acknowledges the Word of God, which is contained in the Scriptures of the Old and New Testaments, to be the supreme rule of faith and life'. On the face of it, these words seem to be a fairly straightforward statement of the duty of the Church to stand under God's truth as written in Scripture, but much has been made of the phrase 'contained in'. Many liberally-minded people have claimed that that phrase means that 'the Word of God' is to be found within the pages of the Bible but these pages may 'contain' other things also.[3]

[1] The phrase 'as understood by Traditionalists' implies that there are other ways of understanding the teaching of Scripture on this matter, whereas the Report had already conceded that 'every single reference to homosexual acts in the entire Bible is negative and condemnatory'.

[2] *Reports 2013*, page 20/15; section 1.5.3.

[3] Cf. the liberal preface to a reading from Scripture, 'Listen for the Word of God', as opposed to the traditional and proper preface, 'Hear the Word of God.'

The word 'contained' is found in the first chapter of the Westminster Confession of Faith; the second paragraph of that chapter reads, 'Under the name of Holy Scripture, or the Word of God written, are now contained all the books of the Old and New Testament.' However, it would be fanciful to imagine that when the Confession was drawn up anyone would have entertained for a moment the idea that God's word is merely to be found somewhere within the pages of the Old and New Testaments. It is only in more recent times (since the advent of 'higher criticism') that such language has been used as 'a subterfuge and an escape clause'.[1]

Writing on the subject of the authority of Scripture, David Torrance regards the liberal interpretation of 'contained in' as 'an attack on the Word of God from within the Church':

> It would seem that some people of a liberal persuasion are attempting to impose upon the present Church a wrong and liberal interpretation of the Bible, which is alien to the apostolic faith. An unbiased interpretation of Church history should make this clear. The Westminster Fathers used the word 'contain' because they wished to affirm that as the Word of God the Bible embraces the Old and New Testaments and they were wishing to exclude from the Bible as God's Word, the books of the Apocrypha. They were also wishing to distinguish the Bible from every other book and affirm its uniqueness. They did not wish to affirm or suggest that parts of the Bible are not the Word of God.[2]

The orthodox view was expressed by J. C. Ryle when he wrote in the 1870s, 'I hold that the Scripture not only *contains* the Word of God, but *is* the Word of God.'[3] The implication of this

[1] Francis Lyall, *Of Presbyters and Kings* (Aberdeen University Press, 1980), 74.

[2] David W. Torrance in *Embracing Truth*, D. W. Torrance & J. Stein, eds., (Handsel Press, 2012), 73-74. He also writes, 'Today the Reformers if alive would wish to resist those who believe that the Bible only "contains" the Word of God, and that some parts are not inspired and therefore not the Word of God' (p. 66). Interestingly, *Embracing Truth* was excluded by an Edinburgh bookshop on the grounds that the shop's managers operated an 'inclusive policy'!

[3] Quoted by Iain H. Murray in 'How Scotland Lost Its Hold of the Bible', *The Banner of Truth, August-September 2015*, 18. Murray writes, 'When you are

statement is that people were already (long before the 1929 union of the Church of Scotland and the United Free Church) saying that the Word was only 'contained in' the Bible, and in recent times this 'contained in' has been used to drive a coach and horses through the orthodoxy to which Ryle referred.

And how did we come from what the Confession incontrovertibly meant by the phrase to this loose use of it which has given rise to the disastrous situation in today's Church of Scotland?

In 1843 the Church of Scotland was split, with some leaving to form the Free Church of Scotland (or, as they preferred, the Church of Scotland Free). Later, in 1900, the Free Church and the United Presbyterian Church joined together to form the United Free Church, which in turn united with the Church of Scotland in 1929. The First Article of the united denomination stated that 'the Church of Scotland receives the Word of God which is contained in the Scriptures of the Old and New Testaments as its supreme rule of faith and life.' Clearly, in 1900 and in 1921 no-one would have considered the possibility of inducting people in active homosexual relationships as ministers, but the loose understanding of the word 'contained' opened a door which would eventually allow liberals to argue for such a move. Iain Murray suggests:

> Article 1 had to be drawn up in language permitting the ambiguous usage of 'contained' because numbers of the leaders and teachers in the United Free Church, with which it (the Church of Scotland) wanted to unite, openly rejected the old belief. ... the union of 1929 could not have been effected without wording that permitted compromise over the authority of Scripture.[1]

The chickens have come home to roost! In the early part of the twenty-first century the door has been opened wide to allow that which Scripture prohibits – all from the little phrase 'contained in'.

carrying home a bag of shopping, you may tell me that it contains potatoes. You may mean that you are only carrying potatoes, or, perhaps, potatoes along with some other items. The promoters of the New Apologetic deliberately made use of this ambiguity' (p. 17).

[1] *Ibid.*, 18.

So when people asked how the 2009 General Assembly's approval of the induction of a homosexual minister could be reconciled with the Church's professed adherence to Scripture, the ground had been prepared for liberals to say in effect, 'Oh but the Church never said that *all* Scripture is the word of God.'

In the 'Articles Declaratory of the Constitution of the Church of Scotland in Matters Spiritual', Clause V says:

> This Church has the inherent right, free from interference by civil authority, but under the safeguards for deliberate action and legislation provided by the Church itself, to frame or adopt its subordinate standards, to declare the sense in which it understands its Confession of Faith, to modify the forms of expression therein, or to formulate other doctrinal statements, and to define the relation thereto of its office-bearers and members, but always in agreement with the Word of God and the fundamental doctrines of the Christian Faith contained in the said Confession, of which agreement the Church shall be sole judge, and with due regard to liberty of opinion in points which do not enter into the substance of the Faith.[1]

On the one hand, this statement makes the proper claim that the Church itself must determine its beliefs without interference from the state or any other body. On the other hand, the statement leaves leeway for the Church to 'declare the sense in which it understands its Confession', to decide what is fundamental and what is not, and to declare what does or does not agree with the word of God.

As an aside, it would be interesting to know what answer would be given by members of the ecclesiastical establishment if they were asked where the rules of the Church of Scotland are to be found.

[1] See J. T. Cox, *Practice and Procedure in the Church of Scotland* (Church of Scotland, 1976), 391. It is notoriously true that there has been much vagueness about points which do or do not 'enter into the substance of the Faith'. When Article 1 says that the Church of Scotland 'avows the fundamental doctrines of the Catholic faith founded (on the Word of God)', this leaves open the question of whether there are some doctrines that are 'fundamental' and some that are not, and claims that the Church has authority to adjudicate on that issue.

If they were to answer, as they well might, that the Church's rules and regulations are contained in the Acts of the General Assembly, one can be sure that they would *not* mean that the regulations are contained somewhere in there; if someone argued against compliance with a particular rule on the ground that it was not of the substance of the regulations, that argument would receive short shrift! The assertion that the regulations are contained in the Acts of Assembly is taken to mean that the Acts of Assembly *in their entirety* are the accepted rules of the General Assembly and therefore of the Church of Scotland.

To suppose that we can pick and choose which parts of the Bible we accept and which parts we reject or ignore, is to elevate our selves and our own judgement above the Bible and thereby reject the authority of God's word. It is no longer the Bible we believe but ourselves! As R. B. Kuiper stated bluntly: 'That the Word of God is in the Bible is a half-truth which frequently implies a falsehood. The truth of the matter is that the Bible is the Word of God.'[1]

We would do well to take to heart Martin Luther's famous challenge when he said that God's call is for faithfulness, not only in general terms but specifically at the point which is under attack at any given time; as we say nowadays, 'where the rubber hits the road'. The form in which it is usually quoted is:

> If I profess with the loudest voice and clearest exposition every portion of the Word of God except precisely that little point which the world and the devil are at that moment attacking, I am not confessing Christ, however boldly I may be professing Him. Where the battle rages there the loyalty of the soldier is proved; and to be steady on all the battle front besides, is mere flight and disgrace if he flinches at that point.[2]

[1] Article, *Scriptural Preaching*, in *Westminster Theological Seminary Symposium, The Infallible Word* (Presbyterian and Reformed Publishing, 1946), 229.

[2] Words found in a nineteenth-century novel, *The Chronicles of the Schoenberg Cotta Family* by Elizabeth Rundle Charles (Thomas Nelson, 1864).

The challenge is clear. It is all very well to assert every aspect of Christianity that is uncontroverted, but our calling is to stand firm everywhere, including the aspects of biblical truth which may be unpopular at any given time. This is why we have had to give so much attention to the particular matter of homosexual practice. It is not that evangelicals are obsessed with homosexuality (as is sometimes alleged) – but, as Melanie Phillips has pointed out (in words quoted earlier) homosexuality is 'the key area where Christians run up against social libertarianism in the public square', and we could add, 'in the Church'.

Arguments

In what follows, we give brief comments on some of the arguments that have been advanced against the so-called traditionalist view.

• It is claimed that *Jesus* did not say anything about homosexuality, with the implication that the matter cannot therefore be very important. In response, we would say that it is absurd to think that any first-century Jewish rabbi would deny what is written in the Scriptures or give any kind of approval to homosexual practice: certain things could be taken for granted. In any case, there are many things that Jesus did not say (for example, he did not refer to incest or violence against women) and the argument from silence is not a good or logical one. More will be said about Jesus' attitude to Scripture in chapter 5.

• It is claimed that the Bible makes no distinction between homosexual orientation and homosexual practice and that it did not know of the existence of stable and committed same-sex relationships. Actually, stable homosexual relationships *were* known in Roman times, but the response to this assertion must be that it is homosexual practice the Bible prohibits. The controversy within the Church is not about same-sex attraction, and it is right to salute the resolve and commitment of people who seek to be obedient to what God has said, whether it pleases them or not. We are all called, in different ways, to deny self, take up our cross, and follow Jesus (Mark 8:34).

• It is argued that the Bible proscribes pederasty rather than homosexuality *per se* – an argument that has no foundation and is an example of *eisegesis* (the practice of reading into the text something that is not there).

• It is argued that some biblical relationships were homosexual in nature. The friendship of David and Jonathan is often referred to in this regard and David's mournful words on Jonathan's death cited: 'Your love to me was extraordinary, surpassing the love of women' (2 Sam. 1:26). Are these words not an indication that a homosexual relationship existed between the two men? One is reminded of Robert Gagnon's comment in which he claims that such arguments are 'specious connections made by people desperate to find the slightest shred of support for homosexual practice in the Bible'.[1]

• It is said that some ministers in the past have denied fundamental doctrines – the virgin birth, the resurrection of Christ, the deity of Christ – and so, liberals ask, why all the fuss about *this* issue? The answer is (a) that such rejections of orthodox biblical truth are indeed very serious and the Church ought to have taken action on such matters and (b) that the issue now is more serious because the Church itself has decided to approve what Scripture condemns. It is bad enough when individual ministers step out of line – it is infinitely worse when the Church, as a body and in deliberate choice, acts against its own foundations in the word of God.

• Others ask why people should take the radical step of leaving the Church over this issue when they did not leave over such a matter as that of the ordination of women to the ministry, which

[1] *The Bible and Homosexual Practice*, as quoted in *Reports to the General Assembly* 2013, 20/80

seems to be prohibited by certain passages of Scripture. This is another matter, but it can be argued that certain passages do seem to leave open the possibility of a more positive attitude toward women in ministerial roles, though not in leadership (Acts 21:9; 1 Cor. 11:5). In the matter of homosexual practice, however, the Bible gives no grounds at all for a positive attitude; there can be no debate about it.

• Some argue that evangelical resistance to the acceptance of homosexual practice is akin to the resistance many showed towards the abolition of slavery. However, those who argue like this overlook the fact that it was evangelicals who campaigned for that abolition. Also, it may have taken far too long for people to work out the implications of Scripture on the issue, but that is no argument for making further mistakes.

• Another line of argument refers to other things condemned by the Bible which we now ignore, such as the wearing of garments made of two materials (Lev. 19:19). Clearly there are different kinds of law in the Old Testament (ceremonial, civil and moral),[1] some of which were specific to ancient Israel; the regulations about the sacrifices, for example, have been fulfilled in and by Christ and they remain in the Bible as pointers to him and as aids to understanding what he has done for his people. The laws against homosexual practice are part of the moral law and do not depend on Leviticus alone.

• Liberals sometimes suggest that it is only a few (extremist) evangelicals who oppose the induction of practising homosexuals. But they forget that opposition to homosexual practice has been the teaching of almost all religions and even of non-religious people throughout the centuries. A general practitioner of medicine wrote:

> The success of the homosexual lobby, representing less than

[1] This distinction is drawn out in paragraphs 3, 4, and 5 of Chapter XIX of the Westminster Confession.

> 2% of the population, outstrips the moon landings as one of the wonders of this [twentieth] century. They have, without any evidence to speak of, persuaded most of the civilised world (and many in the church) that a self-evidently unnatural practice has actually been the victim of unnatural prejudice. This flies in the face of the evidence of reproductive biology, sexual physiology, epidemiology and sociology.[1]

That 'success' is seen in the remarkably widespread acceptance of homosexual practice as natural and good. 'A culture that once frowned upon certain sexual practices now frowns upon those who frown upon them.'[2]

Fuller responses to these and other issues can, of course, be found elsewhere.[3]

And, before moving on to the fundamental question of the Bible's authority, it is interesting to find the frank assessment of Sam Allberry in his helpful little book on same-sex attraction. He is a Christian pastor who experiences same-sex attraction and has come to the conclusion that the godly choice facing all of us is between monogamous heterosexual marriage and celibacy. There is *no third way*; having examined the Bible's teaching he concludes, 'In each instance where the Bible directly addresses homosexual behaviour it is to condemn it.'[4]

Such a conclusion is all the more significant in light of Allberry's own painful experience. He also considers the question of whether homosexual practice is something on which Christians can simply

[1] Dr Jon Garvey: article in *Prophecy Today*, October 1998, 27. Similarly, political commentator Mark Steyn wrote in *Chicago Sun Times* (13 July 2013) that the social change which has taken place within little more than the span of one lifetime is 'one of the most remarkable victories ever achieved by any minority group in the Western world. A minority that didn't even exist in a formal sense a century ago has managed to overwhelm and overhaul a universal social institution thousands of years old.'

[2] Ravi Zacharias, *Why Jesus?* (Faith Words, 2012), xiii.

[3] E.g. R. Gagnon, *The Bible and Homosexual Practice* (Abingdon Press, 2001); Thomas E. Schmidt, *Straight & Narrow?* (IVP, 1995); eds. Torrance & Stein, *Embracing Truth*.

[4] Sam Allberry, *Is God Anti-Gay?* (Good Book Company, 2013), 36.

'agree to differ'. We do in fact agree to differ on some things (for example, the subjects of baptism) and in Romans 14:1 Paul refers to 'disputable matters' (NIV; the Greek word used in the original is related to our English word 'dialogue'), but Allberry goes on to note that Scripture sees homosexual practice as a gospel issue:

> Paul talks about homosexual practice in the context of warning his readers that the unrighteous will not enter the kingdom of God (1 Cor. 6:9). In this category he includes those who practise homosexuality. ... It is not the same order of disagreement as Christians have over, say, baptism, or the practice of certain spiritual gifts.

This chapter has given brief attention to the Bible's teaching. In previous ages, this would have been an end of the matter. If the Bible said a thing, that settled it. For most of our contemporaries, however, it is not enough to simply say, 'The Bible says ...' It is a characteristic of our modern times to ask the 'So what?' question.

This is obviously the case in society at large, with many people consigning the Bible to a library shelf marked, 'Books of Historical Interest'. However, it is also true within the professing church, and this matter is really the watershed issue between evangelical Christianity and liberalism.

> The words 'it is written', or a similar phrase, appear around ninety times in the New Testament. These three words (one word in Greek, *gegraptai*) settled matters for Jesus and the apostles. If Scripture said it, then God said it. They regarded the Bible as God's own word. Through it he speaks. To it Christians listen. Its teaching Christians believe. Its commands Christians obey. Its pages Christians love.[1]

Same-Sex Attraction

Returning to the distinction between same-sex attraction and homosexual acts, *Walking with Gay Friends*[2] is a helpful book

[1] Sinclair B. Ferguson, *From the Mouth of God* (Banner of Truth Trust, 2014), 3.
[2] Alex Tylee, *Walking with Gay Friends* (IVP, 2007), 42.

written by a Christian who struggles with the experience of same-sex attraction. The book helps Christians to know how to show love to homosexual friends and how to share the gospel with them. The book features many real-life stories. One such tells of 'Andy', who wrote about how he had considered all manner of approaches to the interpretation and application of the Bible's teaching on homosexual relationships.

> Even though I wanted to agree with the liberal side of the debate – I wanted to be able to say that the Bible's authority did not say that loving gay relationships were wrong – I couldn't. It is as clear as day: what the Bible says is that any sex outside marriage[1] is wrong, because it is a rejection of God's plan for sex. ... I saw that the choice was either to accept the Bible's authority or to reject it. The option to mess around with the Bible and to make it say what I wanted was simply not open to me; I wanted to live with integrity. This was the crucial choice. I knew that I didn't have the authority to tell God how I should live. The choice was a great cost, but it was the right one: I chose to trust the Bible as God's word.

This choice is the crux of the matter. The footnote against Romans 1:26 in the English Standard Version Study Bible comments, 'Not only homosexual acts but also homosexual passions or desires are dishonourable before God.' We may recall the Lord's comment on the seventh commandment in Matthew 5:27-28:

> You have heard that it was said, 'You shall not commit adultery.' But I say to you that everyone who looks at a woman with lustful intent has already committed adultery with her in his heart.

He presses the matter beyond the outward act to the inner desire, the choice of what to do with the temptation that presents itself. He bids people say 'No' to the temptation, to turn away

[1] This was written before politicians took it on themselves to 'redefine' marriage (as if they could!) to allow men to marry men and women to marry women. This (literally) non-sensical political decision makes no difference to the truth, and 'Andy's' words refer to marriage properly defined as the permanent, exclusive, and public commitment of one man and one woman.

from it. It is a specific application of his word about denying self (Mark 8:34); the word means saying 'No' to our selfish desires and choosing rather to do what is pleasing in God's sight.

And what applies to heterosexual desire also applies to homosexual desire. 'Andy', in the testimony above, speaks of that choice, the choice to turn from what God forbids. Alex Tylee comments:

> Even with the possibility of genetic influence, we cannot therefore conclude that something is part of God's will. A hereditary tendency towards alcohol addiction does not mean that it was God's will for a person to become an alcoholic. Genes too are affected by the Fall, and so genetic dispositions do not make us morally exempt from culpability.[1]

Whatever the temptation may be, the Bible bids us resist the devil (James 4:7). It tells us to 'Flee from sexual immorality' (1 Cor. 6:18) and gives us a graphic instance of it in the story of Joseph who literally fled from temptation at great cost to himself (Gen. 39:12). It is when the temptation is entertained and harboured in the heart that it becomes the 'dishonourable passion' of Romans 1:26. To use the graphic illustration attributed to Martin Luther: 'We cannot help birds flying over our heads but we can prevent them from building their nests in our hair.'

But why? Why are our choices in response to temptation so important? Why, indeed, does it matter what the Bible says?

[1] Tylie, *Walking with Gay Friends*, 51.

5

'Scripture Cannot Be Broken'

'IT is not overstating the case at all', according to an expositor of the theology of Princeton's B. B Warfield, 'to say that the doctrine and character of Scripture were *the* issue of Warfield's day.'[1] The same could be said of these more recent days in the turmoil of Church of Scotland debates. We have considered, albeit briefly, what the Bible says about homosexual practice, but the question is: So what? It may be generally agreed that the Bible proscribes homosexual behaviour, but the obvious riposte of liberals and unbelievers is: 'But why should twenty-first-century people be bound by a book that was written long ago and in a world very different from our own?' Should we yield to the temptation to 'let personal experience trump revealed truth'?[2]

In this chapter we turn to that central question of *why* we should pay heed to the words of Scripture and why the church, if it is to be a *real* church, must adhere to the teaching of the Book – this Bible that centres in the One who said (in the words of the title of this chapter), 'Scripture cannot be broken' (John 10:35).

The truth and relevance of Christianity as a whole is bound up with this question of the truthfulness, reliability, and authority of the Bible. As Ravi Zacharias has written:

> There is absolutely no doubt that the Christian message stands or falls upon the authenticity or spuriousness of the Bible. Knowing

[1] Zaspel, *The Theology of B. B. Warfield*, 111.

[2] Ed Shaw, *The Plausibility Problem* (IVP, 2015), 156. Ed Shaw, who experiences same-sex attraction but is committed to what the Bible says, observes: 'This is a contemporary habit, but it is not the way to reconstruct Christian ethics.'

> it be to be God's Word, millions across history have staked their lives upon it. Destiny-defining trust has been placed in it. Graveside hope has been based upon it. Extraordinary good has been spread because of it. The characters of nations have been built upon it. With equal intensity others have sought to expel it, and wrong-headed zeal has caused untold evil in its name. There is no book in history that has been so studied, so used, and so abused as the Holy Bible. … Nothing is more defining for all of life than to ask the question: 'Has God spoken and can we know that truth?'[1]

At certain times the Bible has been regarded as a dangerous and subversive book. David F. Wright referred, for example, to the 1528 martyrdom of Patrick Hamilton who had been found guilty of believing that it was lawful for ordinary people to read the Bible. Later, an Act of 1536 banned the English Bible and a minister of the Scottish parish of Dollar was burned at the stake in front of Edinburgh Castle in 1539 for his defiance of this ruling.[2] These were terrible times, but the estimation of the Bible as a dangerous book entertained by some in those days contrasts greatly with the disdain and contempt in which the Bible is held by many now.

The importance of the Bible is illustrated by the fact that the very first of the thirty-three chapters of the Westminster Confession of Faith is headed 'Of the Holy Scriptures.' This priority in subject selection conveys the message that the teaching of Scripture is foundational to everything else in the Christian faith. If the truthfulness, reliability, and authority of the Bible were to be undermined, then everything would be 'up for grabs' and open to argument and re-moulding according to the desires and whims of its readers.

The Confession, in the last paragraph of its opening chapter, says,

> The supreme Judge, by which all controversies of religion are to be determined, and all decrees of councils, opinions of ancient

[1] In Foreword: A. Orr-Ewing, *Why Trust the Bible?* (IVP, 2005), 8-10.

[2] D. F. Wright, 'The Bible in the Scottish Reformation', in ed. D. F. Wright, *The Bible in Scottish Life and Literature* (Saint Andrew Press, 1988), 162.

> writers, doctrines of men, and private spirits, are to be examined, and in whose sentence we are to rest, can be no other but the Holy Spirit speaking in the scriptures.

The 'proof texts' given for this section include Matthew 22:29, in which we hear Jesus saying to some Sadducees, 'You are wrong, because you know neither the Scriptures nor the power of God', and in verse 31, 'Have you not read what was said to you by God?' We are also referred to Paul's words in Acts 28:25 about the way in which the Holy Spirit spoke to the fathers through Isaiah the prophet, and in Ephesians 2:20 about the church as 'built on the foundation of the apostles and prophets, Christ Jesus himself being the cornerstone'.

Nigel Cameron has written:

> The question of the authority of the Bible has been at centre of the crisis of belief which has enveloped the church for more than a century, since that which holds the most central place in the practice of the Church's faith has become the object of the most serious doubt. The early Christians inherited from their Jewish forebears a belief in Holy Scripture as the Word of God. For them this first referred to the Old Testament, but soon also to the writings of the New, as is already evident in II Peter 3:15-16.[1]

In that passage Peter refers to some things in the writings of 'our beloved brother Paul' which are hard to understand and which some people were twisting '... to their own destruction, as they do the other Scriptures'. That last phrase clearly implies that, when Peter was writing, Paul's words were already regarded as divinely inspired and authoritative.

In considering the question of that authority, and why the church should be bound by it, we shall refer to (1) the testimony of the ages, (2) the testimony of the Bible itself, (3) the testimony of Jesus and (4) the testimony of the Holy Spirit.

[1] *The Pulpit Bible, in Pulpit & People*, ed. N. Cameron & S. B. Ferguson (Rutherford House, 1986), 29.

(1) The Testimony of the Ages

One of the most remarkable things about the Bible is its survival. It has been attacked, critiqued, insulted, and proscribed as no other book, yet still it stands, which gives eloquent testimony to the truth of Isaiah 40:8 – 'The grass withers, the flower fades, but the word of our God will stand for ever.'

The text which has been taken as a kind of motto-text of the Presbyterian churches is well chosen, with the emblem of the burning bush and the words of Exodus 3:2 about the bush which Moses saw: '*Nec Tamen Consumebatur*' – 'Yet it was not consumed.' This has been the story not only of the church but also of the Bible. It has been forbidden, it has been burned – sometimes literally – but it has never been consumed.

Critics have attacked its accuracy, questioned its veracity, and alleged that it is full of contradictions. Others have acted as if we are at liberty to choose which parts to accept and which to reject and jettison. Nigel Cameron refers to this selective use of the Bible. He shows the inconsistency of those who are happy to reject some parts of the Bible and yet rely on its other parts for their beliefs:

> The question remains whether the rejection of the authority of Scripture in particular areas does not entail the rejection of its authority as a whole. That is to say, in those areas in which its teaching is accepted, is it accepted because of the authority of Scripture, or is it accepted because in these particular cases the teaching of Scripture happens to coincide with positions taken up for other reasons? ... It is incumbent upon those who dissent from the historic doctrine of Biblical authority to explain the logic of their position. In particular, they must be able to explain how their own doubts about the Bible relate to the confidence which they invite others to have in it at points where they accept its teaching, which they desire to commend.[1]

Applying that challenge to the contemporary crunch point of homosexual practice, he poses the obvious question:

[1] *Ibid.*, 31-2.

> If it is open to us to reject that condemnation, what of the condemnation of fornication and of adultery? May we now, with as much or as little justification, decide to reject such prohibitions too?

But is the Bible reliable? Can we even trust that what we have is what the original writers set down? F. F. Bruce wrote,

> The evidence for our New Testament writings is ever so much greater than the evidence for many writings of classical authors, the authenticity of which no-one dreams of questioning.[1]

There are approximately 5,000 Greek manuscripts of the New Testament in whole or in part, compared with, for example, nine or ten for Caesar's *Gallic Wars*, the oldest of which was written 900 years after the events it records. This contrasts with

> a papyrus codex containing John 18:31-33 & 37f., now in the John Rylands Library, Manchester, dated on palaeological grounds around A.D. 130, showing that the latest of the four Gospels, which was written, according to tradition, at Ephesus between A.D. 90 and 100, was circulating in Egypt within about forty years of its composition.[2]

And the discovery of the Dead Sea Scrolls in 1947 has added greatly to the evidence for the reliability of the documents in the Old Testament. The scrolls had lain in a cave from A.D. 68 and they include much of Isaiah and fragments from nearly all of the books of the Old Testament. It has been calculated that these fragments are identical with 95% of the same text found in our Bibles, with only minor variations in the other 5%.

Other discoveries have also given further reasons to be confident about the reliability of the biblical documents. For example, Acts 18:12 mentions Gallio, the proconsul of Achaia, who was a brother of the well-known Roman philosopher and statesman Seneca. Because of this family connection Gallio's career was well documented in secular sources, but for a long time sceptics thought

[1] F. F. Bruce, *The New Testament Documents* (IVF, 1943), 15.

[2] *Ibid.*, 17.

it unlikely that the title of the office he held in Achaia, used by Luke in that passage in Acts, fitted in with what was known of his career drawn from other sources – that is, until an inscription was found in Delphi, revealing that Gallio was indeed 'proconsul of Achaia', and supplying the date, A.D. 51–52, which also helped scholars date Paul's missionary journeys.

Clearly a book like this can only touch on such matters but it can be confidently asserted that the documents we have in our Bibles have been accurately transmitted.[1]

And if people ask who decided which of all the books in circulation were to be regarded as authoritative scripture, we respond by saying that the early church did not so much *decide* as *recognise* which books were inspired. It is a remarkable thing that, without any ecclesiastical machinery to enforce a decision, practically the whole church came to recognise the same twenty-seven books as authoritative. And so:

> When at last a Church Council – the Synod of Hippo in A.D. 393 – listed the twenty-seven books of the New Testament, it did not confer upon them any authority which they did not already possess, but simply recorded their previously established canonicity.[2]

It was not a case of a group of people randomly deciding which books to accept, or of people with vested interests making such

[1] Cf. 'As well as the discovery of early fragments of the New Testament, the writings of the church Fathers provide us with good evidence for a short period of time between the events themselves and the Gospels which describe them. For example, the Epistle of Clement to the Corinthians (dated A.D. 95) cites verses from the Gospels, Acts, Romans, 1 Corinthians, Ephesians, Titus, Hebrews and 1 Peter.' Also, the abrupt ending of Acts probably means that Luke was writing before Paul's appearance before Caesar (c. A.D. 62–63) and no New Testament book refers to the destruction of the temple in A.D. 70. There are 'thousands of quotations ... dispersed throughout the writings of the church Fathers. In fact there are 86,000 quotations – this means that if all the ancient New Testament manuscripts were somehow to disappear overnight, it would still be possible to reconstruct the entire New Testament with quotations from the church fathers, with the exception of about twenty verses!' Orr-Ewing, *Why Trust the Bible?*, 41-2.

[2] F. F. Bruce, *The Books and the Parchments* (Pickering & Inglis, 1984), 117. (The words canon/canonicity derive from the Greek word for a reed, which was used as a measuring rod.)

decisions. It is not that the church gave us the Bible, but that the Bible gave us the church and it is God who has given us the Bible. As Jim Packer has written, 'The church no more created the canon than Newton created the law of gravity.'[1] It was widely recognised that these sixty-six books had the ring of truth.[2]

That testimony to the Bible's ring of truth has been echoed time and again through the centuries, and the effect and influence of the Bible is another pointer to its divine inspiration and authority. John Stott wrote eloquently of this effect of God's word. Christian people

> founded schools, hospitals, and refuges for the outcast. Later still they abolished the slave trade and freed the slaves, and they improved the conditions of workers in mills and mines, and of prisoners in gaols. They protected children from commercial exploitation in the factories of the West and from ritual prostitution in the temples of the East. Today they bring leprosy sufferers both the compassion of Jesus and modern methods of reconstructive surgery and rehabilitation. They care for the blind and the deaf, the orphaned and the widowed, the sick and the dying. They get alongside junkies, and stay alongside them during the traumatic period of withdrawal. They set themselves against racism and political oppression. They get involved in the urban scene, the inner city, the slums and ghettoes, and raise their protest against the inhuman conditions in which so many are doomed to live. They seek in whatever way they can to express their solidarity with the poor and hungry, the deprived and disadvantaged.[3]

Of course no-one would claim that only Christians have effected positive change in the world or that Christians have always or consistently lived up to the standards set in Scripture. A New Age

[1] J. I. Packer, *Under God's Word* (Marshall, Morgan & Scott, 1980), 132.

[2] Which was the title of a paperback by J. B. Phillips, *Ring of Truth* (Hodder & Stoughton, 1967) – in the preface of which he wrote, 'I do not care what the *avant-garde* scholars say; I do very much care what God says and does. I have therefore felt compelled to write this book. It is my testimony to the historicity and reliability of the New Testament' (p. 8).

[3] J. Stott, *Issues Facing Christians Today* (Marshall Morgan & Scott, 1984), 19.

writer made the blunt statement, 'Christianity has not been very Christian',[1] and we cannot deny that things have often been done in the name of Christ which have dishonoured that name in the eyes of the world (cf. Rom. 2:24). And at the personal level no Christian can claim to be all that he or she is called to be; every failure in discipleship is a constant, painful reminder that God's church is 'a work in progress'.

At the same time, however, the basic fact cannot be denied that the Bible's influence has been immense and ennobling. In so many ways history has demonstrated that the Bible is no ordinary book.

(2) The Testimony of the Bible Itself

What about the testimony of the Bible itself, the claims it makes. Its claims are very striking.

• Old Testament writers frequently use such expressions as, 'God said' and 'The word of the LORD came.' For example, in Jonah 3:1 we are told, 'The word of the LORD came to Jonah the second time ...' It was not that an idea came into Jonah's head; the emphasis is that God spoke to him. How? We are not given details about the mechanics of the matter – whether God brought the message to Jonah's mind, or, as elsewhere, made his message known through dreams or visions, such as that experienced by Isaiah when, he records, 'I heard the voice of the Lord saying, "Whom shall I send, and who will go for us?" Then I said, "Here I am! Send me"' (Isa. 6:8).

• David testified in 2 Samuel 23:2 (NIV), 'The Spirit of the LORD spoke through me', and, centuries later, Peter claimed, 'The Scripture had to be fulfilled, which the Holy Spirit spoke beforehand through the mouth of David (concerning Judas)' (Acts 1:16).

• Paul begins his letter to the Romans by referring to the 'gospel of God' as something which he 'promised beforehand through his prophets in the holy Scriptures' (Rom. 1:1-2).

[1] Quoted in John Drane, *Evangelism for a New Age* (Marshall Pickering, 1994), 209.

• Paul equated what Scripture says with what God says, as in Romans 9:17 where he writes, 'For the Scripture says to Pharaoh ...' The apostle is referring to a paragraph in Exodus which is introduced by the words, 'Then the LORD said to Moses ...' (Exod. 9:13ff.).

• In Galatians 1:11-12 Paul wrote, 'The gospel that was preached by me is not man's gospel. For I did not receive it from any man, nor was I taught it, but I received it through a revelation of Jesus Christ'; and in 1 Corinthians 2:13, he wrote, 'We impart this in words not taught by human wisdom but taught by the Spirit.'[1]

• 2 Timothy 3:16: 'All Scripture is breathed out by God and profitable for teaching, for reproof, for correction, and for training in righteousness, that the man of God may be complete, equipped for every good work.'

• 1 Peter 1:10-12: 'Concerning this salvation, the prophets who prophesied about the grace that was to be yours searched and enquired carefully, enquiring what person or time *the Spirit of Christ in them* was indicating when he predicted the sufferings of Christ and the subsequent glories. *It was revealed to them* that they were serving not themselves but you, in the things that have now been announced to you through those who preached the good news to you by the Holy Spirit sent from heaven, things into which angels long to look.'

• 2 Peter 1:21: 'No prophecy was ever produced by the will of man, but men spoke from God as they were carried along by the Holy Spirit.' The individual writers – Jeremiah, David, Moses, *etc.*

[1] In the last chapter of 2 Corinthians Paul referred to people who were questioning his authority (verse 3: 'you seek proof that Christ is speaking in me'). He had said at the very beginning of the epistle that he was an apostle 'by the will of God', and he was not motivated by self-concern but concern for the honour of his Master. He would put up with insults against himself, but, as James Denny argued, when people challenged his apostolic authority they were really challenging the authority of Christ by whose will Paul was an apostle.

– wrote in a way that was characteristic of their individual styles and personalities, yet this verse makes the astonishing claim that all the prophets wrote had its origin in God and was produced under the superintendence of the Holy Spirit.

• In 2 Peter 3:16 we find a reference to people who were twisting some of the things written by Paul 'as they do the other Scriptures' – clearly treating the writings of Paul as authoritative scripture.

• The last book of the Bible is introduced as the 'revelation of Jesus Christ, which God gave him to show to his servants the things that must soon take place. He made it known by sending his angel to his servant John, who bore witness to the word of God and to the testimony of Jesus Christ' (Rev. 1:1-2). The apostle John testified: 'I was in the Spirit on the Lord's day, and I heard behind me a loud voice' (Rev. 1:10) – and in what follows we see the risen Lord dictating seven letters to John which are to be sent to the seven churches in the province of Asia. Each letter concludes with the same message, 'He who has an ear, let him hear what the Spirit says to the churches.'

In these ways, the Bible itself claims to be a unique book, the product of revelation. The claim is consistently made that, whoever the human authors were, it was God himself who breathed out his word into their hearts and minds.

It should also be noted that in Scripture solemn warnings are given about false claims to inspiration and false prophets are roundly condemned. Consider, for example, the extended treatment of God's judgement upon the false prophets of Judah and Jerusalem in Jeremiah's day (Jer. 23):

> Concerning the prophets: My heart is broken within me; all my bones shake ... Their course is evil, and their might is not right. 'Both prophet and priest are ungodly; even in my house I have found their evil, declares the LORD. Therefore their way shall be to them like slippery paths in the darkness, into which they shall be driven and fall, for I will bring disaster upon them in the year of their punishment, declares the LORD.

But in the prophets of Jerusalem I have seen a horrible thing ... they strengthen the hands of evildoers, so that no one turns from his evil; all of them have become like Sodom to me, and its inhabitants like Gomorrah.'

Therefore thus says the LORD of hosts concerning the prophets: 'Behold, I will feed them with bitter food and give them poisoned water to drink, for from the prophets of Jerusalem ungodliness has gone out into all the land.'

Thus says the LORD of hosts: 'Do not listen to the words of the prophets who prophesy to you, filling you with vain hopes. They speak visions of their own minds, not from the mouth of the LORD. They say continually to those who despise the word of the LORD, "It shall be well with you"; and to everyone who stubbornly follows his own heart, they say, "No disaster shall come upon you."'

For who among them has stood in the council of the LORD to see and to hear his word, or who has paid attention to his word and listened?

'I did not send the prophets, yet they ran; I did not speak to them, yet they prophesied. But if they had stood in my council, then they would have proclaimed my words to my people, and they would have turned them from their evil way, and from the evil of their deeds ...

I have heard what the prophets have said who prophesy lies in my name, saying, 'I have dreamed, I have dreamed!' How long shall there be lies in the heart of the prophets who prophesy lies, and who prophesy the deceit of their own heart, who think to make my people forget my name by their dreams that they tell one another, even as their fathers forgot my name for Baal? Let the prophet who has a dream tell the dream, but let him who has my word speak my word faithfully.

How different is the true word of God delivered through his servants the prophets and apostles! Scripture has a self-authenticating character all of its own, as the majestic language of the Westminster Confession says so memorably:

We may be moved and induced by the testimony of the Church to

> a high and reverend esteem of the holy scriptures; and the heavenliness of the matter, the efficacy of the doctrine, the majesty of the style, the consent of all the parts, the scope of the whole (which is to give all glory to God), the full discovery it makes of the only way of man's salvation, the many other incomparable excellencies, and the entire perfection thereof, are arguments whereby it doth abundantly evidence itself to be the word of God.[1]

This self-evidencing character of Scripture is expounded by Jesus himself: 'My teaching is not mine, but his who sent me. If anyone's will is to do God's will, he will know whether the teaching is from God' (John 7:16-17).

And Isaiah passed on God's message: 'My word that goes out from my mouth shall not return to me empty, but it shall accomplish that which I purpose, and shall succeed in the things for which I sent it' (Isa. 55:11).

In all of these references the Bible itself assumes and claims that its words are the words of God. What about Jesus himself?

(3) The Testimony of Jesus

If Christianity centres in Jesus Christ, then it is obviously significant to find out and follow what he says – about Scripture as about all other subjects. If we are called to 'follow him' (Matt. 16:24; John 12:26), then one of the particular ways in which we are called to do so is to receive and believe his teaching about the Scriptures.

And what we find is that Jesus set his seal of authority on the Old Testament Scriptures and provided for the writing of the New Testament Scriptures. 'The high view of Scripture traditionally held by the church was taught by and learned from the Lord Jesus Christ.'[2]

So far as the Old Testament is concerned, it is significant that at the very outset of his ministry Jesus faced Satanic temptation

[1] Westminster Confession of Faith, I.5.
[2] Zaspel, *The Theology of B. B. Warfield*, 131.

by quoting and relying on the words of the Old Testament. When he used the phrase, 'It is written' (Luke 4:4; 4:8; 4:12), the clear implication is that the Scriptures Jesus was quoting were authoritative; if the Scriptures say it, that settles it.

When Jesus said in the Sermon on the Mount, 'Not an iota, not a dot, will pass from the Law until all is accomplished' (Matt. 5:18), there may be debate about what 'accomplished' means, but there can be no argument about what Jesus was clearly saying regarding the Law: it (the Old Testament) is divinely inspired and therefore unbreakable. Obviously the Old Testament Scriptures had particular regulations that were intended to be preparatory and temporary until the coming of Christ. Parts of the Old Testament give detailed regulations, for example, about animal sacrifices, the practice and apparel of the priests who served in the tabernacle, and the New Testament teaches (notably in the Letter to the Hebrews) that such types and shadows and regulations have all been fulfilled in Christ.

In Matthew 19:5 we find the words of Genesis 2:24 quoted by Jesus and directly attributed to God: 'Have you not read that he who created them ... said, "Therefore a man shall leave his father and mother and hold fast to his wife, and the two shall become one flesh"?'

In Matthew 22:31, referring to the words of Exodus 3:6, Jesus challenged the Sadducees, 'Have you not read what was said to you *by God*?'

Similarly in Mark 12:36, referring to the words of Psalm 110, he said, 'David himself, in the Holy Spirit, declared ...'

In John 10:35, he plainly declared, 'Scripture cannot be broken.'

In his encounter with the two disciples on the Emmaus Road, he said, 'Everything written about me in the Law of Moses and the Prophets and the Psalms must be fulfilled' (Luke 24:44).

These verses show us the attitude of Jesus to the Old Testament Scriptures. John Blanchard has written, 'The only "Bible" Jesus had in his day was the Old Testament, but he is recorded as quoting verbatim from it nearly forty times (from thirteen different books) in the course of his teaching, and as referring to it on many other occasions.'[1] Jesus treated the Scriptures as divinely inspired and authoritative and we cannot claim to be true followers and obedient disciples of the Lord Jesus Christ if we refuse to follow his teaching in this foundational matter.

And what of the New Testament? If the Old Testament is authoritative for Christians because Jesus set his seal upon it, what are we to say of the New Testament?

The New Testament finds its centre in the belief that in Jesus Christ the eternal Word became flesh (John 1:14), and it was that Jesus who made provision for the setting down of what was taught *by* him along with what was taught, under the Father's inspiration, *about* him.

Jesus said to his disciples,

> These things I have spoken to you while I am still with you. But the Helper, the Holy Spirit, whom the Father will send in my name, he will teach you all things and bring to your remembrance all that I have said to you (John 14:25-26).

The Holy Spirit guides Christians in all ages, but this promise was addressed specifically to the apostles gathered around Jesus. He was saying that the Holy Spirit would guide them in the writing down of the gospel message. 'In essence, without actually saying it in so many words, Jesus is explaining: "My apostles will write the New Testament."'[2]

Similarly, two chapters later, Jesus said to them,

> When the Spirit of truth comes, he will guide you into all the truth, for he will not speak on his own authority, but whatever he hears he will speak, and he will declare to you the things that are to come. He will glorify me, for he will take what is mine and declare it to you (John 16:13-14).

It is in line with this provision of Jesus himself that two of these disciples would later take care to emphasise the fact that

[1] John Blanchard, *Why Believe the Bible?* (Evangelical Press, 2004), 25.
[2] Ferguson, *From the Mouth of God*, 34.

the Gospel records were not fabrications or old wives' tales. Peter wrote:

> We did not follow cleverly devised myths when we made known to you the power and coming of our Lord Jesus Christ, but we were *eyewitnesses* of his majesty. For when he received honour and glory from God the Father, and the voice was borne to him by the Majestic Glory, 'This is my beloved Son, with whom I am well pleased', we ourselves heard this very voice borne from heaven, for we were with him on the holy mountain (2 Pet. 1:16-18).

And the apostle John wrote:

> That which was from the beginning, which we have *heard*, which we have *seen with our eyes*, which we looked upon and have *touched with our hands*, concerning the word of life – the life was made manifest, and we have seen it, and testify to it and proclaim to you the eternal life, which was with the Father and was made manifest to us – that which we have seen and heard we proclaim also to you (1 John 1:1-3).

Jesus' purpose was that these disciples would, through the inspiration of the Spirit, be enabled to write God's word down for the illumination, instruction and guidance of future generations who had not seen with their own eyes the all-important events that lie at the heart of the message of salvation. These future generations are to 'search the Scriptures', for, as Jesus said, 'it is they that bear witness about me' (John 5:39).

Very striking are the words at the end of the book of Revelation, whether taken as referring only to that last book of the Bible or to the Bible as a whole:

> I warn everyone who hears the words of the prophecy of this book: if anyone adds to them, God will add to him the plagues described in this book, and if anyone takes away from the words of the book of this prophecy, God will take away his share in the tree of life and in the holy city, which are described in this book (Rev. 22:18-19).

So Jesus' seal of authority is found on both the Old Testament and the New Testament Scriptures: they are the word of God. This is the reason why Paul, in writing his first letter to the Thessalonian Christians, could remind them of the reception they had given to the gospel message he had preached during his first visit to their city: 'We thank God constantly for this, that when you received the word of God, which you heard from us, you accepted it not as the word of men but as what it really is, the word of God' (1 Thess. 2:13).

Such is the claim of the apostles of Jesus Christ. Their words are either the most self-promoting hubris or the faithful record of the words and work of the Lord Jesus Christ. Actually, it would be a strange kind of self-promotion, since the Gospels are unsparing in their record of the faults and failings of the disciples. Sometimes they were slow to understand (*e.g.*, John 14:5; Matt. 16:22) and sometimes they completely missed the point (*e.g.*, Luke 9:46; Luke 9:54). If the gospel were all a made-up story, would it have included the story of Peter's denials (Mark 14:66-72), would it (in the culture of that time) have made women the first witnesses of the resurrection (Matt. 28:9), would it have included the scepticism of Thomas (John 20:24-25)?

Another indication of the genuineness of the New Testament documents is their frequent warnings about the cost of following Jesus; the New Testament does not downplay the demanding nature of Christian discipleship in an effort to make the message popular. For example, Luke tells of Paul being stoned almost to death and then, after recovering, encouraging the believers to steadfastness, 'saying that through many tribulations we must enter the kingdom of God' (Acts 14:19-22). Similarly, Peter wrote to his readers, saying: 'Beloved, do not be surprised at the fiery trial when it comes upon you to test you, as though something strange were happening to you. But rejoice insofar as you share Christ's sufferings ...' (1 Pet. 4:12-13). When he wrote that, was he thinking back to the Sermon on the Mount, when Jesus himself said: 'Blessed are you when others revile you and persecute you and utter all kinds of evil against you falsely on my account. Rejoice and be glad, for your reward is great in heaven, for so they persecuted the prophets who were before you' (Matt. 5:11-12)?

Was Jesus a Revisionist?

One other issue may be raised here before we go on to consider the testimony of the Holy Spirit. The debates in the Church of Scotland have referred to 'traditionalist' versus 'revisionist' views, but could it be claimed that Jesus was himself a revisionist? There are a few passages in the Gospels, it might be asserted, where Jesus *appears* to be rejecting the Old Testament. If that were so, could such a rejection of the law be legitimately used by today's revisionists to back up their case for a radical re-interpretation of biblical texts?

As we have seen, Jesus said such things as, 'Scripture cannot be broken' (John 10:35) and, 'It is easier for heaven and earth to pass away than for one dot of the law to become void' (Luke 16:17). But there are other places in the Gospels where it may *look as if* he were repudiating the Old Testament. Did he deny in practice what he taught in theory?

In Matthew 19 Jesus quoted the words of Genesis 2:24 about God's plan for marriage as the permanent union of a man and a woman. When he was then challenged (verse 7) about the Mosaic law which allowed for a certificate of divorce to be granted, Jesus said that divorce was valid on the grounds of sexual unfaithfulness. Again, in the Sermon on the Mount, we find a series of contrasting statements in the form: 'You have heard that it was said ... But I say to you' (Matt. 5:21, 27, 31, 33, 38, 43).

Was Jesus rejecting God's word in the Old Testament? Actually, in each case these statements follow strong words about the abiding authority and relevance of Scripture – for example, 'Until heaven and earth pass away, not an iota, not a dot, will pass from the Law' (Matt. 5:18) – and one can hardly imagine that within a few breaths Jesus would then proceed to repudiate that very law. What the Lord was really doing was bringing out the *true meaning* of the law, in contrast to the false interpretations of the religious leaders of the time.

This is borne out by the details. In the Sermon on the Mount Jesus repeatedly said, 'You have *heard* that it was *said*' – which is different from 'You have *read* what was *written*.' The contrast is between what some were teaching the law said and, on the other hand, what the law really meant.

Take the example of the Law's teaching on divorce: Jesus was not attacking Moses for the provision of a certificate of divorce; rather, he was rejecting the idea that this law of Moses could be used to excuse divorce on any grounds.

Or again, when Jesus referred to oaths (Matt. 5:33), he was not contradicting the Old Testament's proscription of 'swearing falsely' but making the point that his followers are to be people who don't need to swear elaborate oaths.

In the last of the six 'Antitheses', Jesus said, 'You have heard that it was said, "You shall love your neighbour and hate your enemy."' However, that last phrase is not found in the Old Testament; there is in fact a verse that talks about loving the sojourner or stranger (Deut. 10:19). Jesus was arguing against contemporary misunderstandings of what was written in the Old Testament.

Far from being a revisionist in the sense of over-riding the law found in Scripture, Jesus was drawing out its real spiritual significance and challenge. His whole position with regard to this matter can be summed up in these words of his: 'Do not think that I have come to abolish the Law or the Prophets; I have not come to abolish them but to fulfil them' (Matt. 5:17).

Jesus was not a revisionist, and there are no grounds for claiming his support for contemporary desires to re-define the law or alter the Bible's teaching to suit modern preferences.

(4) The Testimony of the Spirit

In his 'upper room discourse' Jesus spoke of the time when the Spirit of truth would come into the hearts of his people. He said that the Spirit would 'glorify me, for he will take what is mine and declare it to you' (John 16:14). These words, addressed originally to the apostles in connection with their writing down the Lord's words, are also true for us who read the Lord's words recorded by the apostles, as Paul reminded the Corinthian believers: 'We have received not the spirit of the world, but the Spirit who is from God, that we might understand the things freely given us by God' (1 Cor. 2:12). As we read the 'words of eternal life' (John 6:68), we have a growing inner conviction that we are reading no ordinary words but the very words of God himself.

Jesus spoke of this inner conviction when he said: 'If anyone's will is to do God's will, he will know whether the teaching is from God' (John 7:17). The Spirit breathes upon the word and brings the truth to light,[1] and we do well to approach the Bible, not with a condescending attitude of superiority, but with the prayerful attitude of the hymn:

> Come, Holy Ghost, for moved by Thee
> The prophets wrote and spoke;
> Unlock the truth, Thyself the key,
> Unseal the sacred Book.
>
> God, through Himself, we then shall know
> If Thou within us shine ...[2]

This does not mean that the authority of Scripture lies solely in our inner conviction, as though the words of the Bible *become* the word of God only when the Holy Spirit illumines the heart and mind. In the first chapter of the Westminster Confession, paragraph 5 comes after paragraph 4! In other words, paragraph 5 speaks about 'the inward work of the Holy Spirit, bearing witness

[1] Hymn by William Cowper (1731–1800).

[2] 'Come, Holy Ghost, our hearts inspire', by Charles Wesley (1707–88).

by and with the word in our hearts', but this comes after the assertion in paragraph 4 that the authority of the Bible depends 'wholly upon God (who is truth itself), the author thereof; and therefore it is to be received, because it is the word of God'. Nonetheless, it is a wonderful thing when the Holy Spirit opens our eyes (Psa. 119:105) so that we *are* inwardly convinced that what we are reading is the very word of God!

An interesting postscript to this section is found in the testimony of Jim Packer who has written of his conversion at Oxford and how he was nurtured by other Christians:

> ... one of the first things that became reality for me in the course of that nurture (by Inter-Varsity people) was what John Calvin later taught me to recognize as the inward witness of the Holy Spirit to the divinity of Holy Scripture. I can still remember the gathering at which I went in, not at all sure that the Bible was the Word of God, and came out absolutely certain that it was, though all that had happened was that one visionary chapter of the Book of Revelation had been reverently expounded. It was not until long after that I found in Calvin the phrase that fits what had happened to me. Calvin said that the Spirit-given certainty that the Bible is the Word of God is something that every Christian experiences. I rejoiced when I read that, for that was what I had experienced. The conviction that the Bible is as divine as it is human has been with me ever since.[1]

Conclusion

All of the things outlined in this chapter – the testimony of the ages, the testimony of the Bible itself, the testimony of Jesus, and the inner testimony of the Spirit – lead to a 'high' view of the inspiration and authority of the Bible. It is not a matter of taking the Bible 'literally' – we know what Jesus meant, for example, when he said, 'I am the vine' (John 15:5), just as we 'get' the force of the reference in Revelation 1:16 to a sword coming from the mouth of the ascended Lord.

[1] *Honouring the Written Word of God* (Regent College ed., 2008), 161.

Nor does this 'high' view of Scripture mean that everything written in the Bible is for emulation; many things are recorded without any implication that they should be repeated or copied (for example, in John 2:15 we are told that Jesus made a whip, but we are not told to go and do likewise; the story of Gideon's fleece in Judges 6:36-40 is another example).

We are not to be tied to any mechanical view of inspiration.

> The Bible says there are 'many ways' (Hebrews 1:1) in which the actual words of the Bible were written. Sometimes God spoke directly to the author, who simply recorded what he heard (Revelation 2:1, 8, 12). At other times the author based much of his writings on interviews and research (Luke 1:1-3). And at other times, the Holy Spirit brought to mind things that Jesus taught (John 14:26). Regardless of the way in which the words came to the authors, they were an expression of them – their personalities, skills, backgrounds, and training. But they were also exactly the words God wanted them to write – the very words that God claims as his own.[1]

Not all parts of Scripture are equally easy to understand and the fact that every part of Scripture is equally inspired does not mean that all are equally 'inspiring' (genealogical lists, for example – although they also have their importance). There are parts of Scripture that we find difficult, but one is often reminded of the remark attributed to Mark Twain that the parts of the Bible which bothered him were not the parts he did not understand but the parts he did understand only too well! The Bible is not always a book of comfort: it comforts the disturbed but also disturbs the comfortable.

We referred earlier to Jesus' words in Matthew 22:29: 'You are wrong, because you know neither the Scriptures nor the power of God.'[2] He was addressing Sadducees who were ridiculing the

[1] W. Grudem, *Christian Beliefs* (Zondervan, 2005), 14.

[2] 'I confess that I find His outspokenness very refreshing. Jesus did not compliment them, as we might have done, on getting hold of an important aspect of the truth, or on contributing a valuable insight to current theological debate. No. They were wrong.' J. Stott, *Christ the Controversialist* (Tyndale Press, 1970), 52.

idea that there was any life after death. They were ignorant of God's inspired word and of his supernatural power. By contrast, Paul could write to Timothy, 'From childhood you have been acquainted with the sacred writings, which are able to make you wise for salvation through faith in Christ Jesus' (2 Tim. 3:15). And he went on to assert, 'All Scripture is breathed out by God.'[1]

The Sadducees who confronted Jesus wanted to make fun of him. They were the rationalists of their day; they would have said that they believed in God, yet they were characterised more by what they did not believe than by what they did. In particular, they did not believe in the resurrection of the body and life eternal (verse 23). They would have dismissed such a notion as a naïve flight of fancy for those not enlightened enough to accept that this life is the only life there is. Matthew 22 is a passage that challenges us as we read it today; do we stand with the Sadducees, breathing the suffocating air of the sceptical secularism that is all around us, or are we among those who believe Jesus' word in his teaching about the life to come?

What he said to the Sadducees was, 'You are wrong, because you know neither the Scriptures nor the power of God.' He also said to them, 'As for the resurrection of the dead, have you not read what was said to you by God?' (Matt. 22:31). He directed them to the Bible which they were supposed to believe and it is the same challenge that comes to us today, whether the issue is that of life after death, homosexual practice, or any other. His diagnosis – *you are wrong because you know neither the Scriptures nor the power of God* – puts its finger on the very problems facing us today.

Jim Jones (1931–78) was an American preacher who founded the People's Temple cult. He was a communist who posed as a Christian preacher. He founded a religious commune in Guyana

[1] The New English Bible illustrates the selective use of the Bible with its tendentious translation, 'Every inspired Scripture has its use for teaching ...', as if we could distinguish between those scriptures that are inspired and those that are not. But that can hardly be regarded as a fair translation of the original words.

and in 1978 led the suicide pact which resulted in the deaths of 909 people including 300 children. Most died from cyanide poisoning, Jones himself from gunshot wounds (presumed to be suicide).

In a filmed dramatisation of the tragedy, Jones was seen preaching and rhetorically asking the congregation, 'Do we trust in ...?' – mentioning various things, and the congregation responded aloud, 'No.' In the end he held up a Bible and asked, 'Is this what we trust in?' When the congregation responded with a loud 'Yes', he repeated it, and then went on to say, 'No! We don't believe in a book; it's the Lord we follow!' The scene then showed him setting the Bible to one side: that was the beginning of the slippery slope that led to the chaos and suicide of all those people.

We cannot separate the Lord from his word. The right attitude is that described by Luke in his account of Paul's second missionary journey. Paul and Silas had left Thessalonica where they had been vilified by their opponents as people who were turning the world upside down (Acts 17:6), and they had gone on to Berea where, Luke tells us, 'These Jews were more noble than those at Thessalonica; they received the word with all eagerness, examining the Scriptures daily to see if these things were so' (Acts 17:11).

The Bereans model for us the truly 'noble' attitude to Scripture: serious attention to it, regular reading of it, and biblical thinking as a result. Luke emphasizes the eagerness of their examination of the Scriptures, using a word that means 'investigate carefully'. He uses the same word in Luke 23:14, where we are told that Pontius Pilate had 'examined' Jesus and found him innocent of any crime. The Bereans were diligent in the way they used their Bibles (the Old Testament at that time); they were not like people who have a Bible somewhere in the house but who never actually read it.

The Bereans used Scripture as a yardstick by which to measure the truth of what Paul was telling them. 'Was the apostle's message biblical?' That was the key question for them. Notice that they did not assess Paul's teaching on the basis of whether it was appealing to their senses, or whether it fitted in with their own way of thinking. Neither did they arrange a focus group in order to consult popular opinion on the matter. 'To the teaching and to the testimony' (Isa. 8:20) was their approach and they are commended for it! And Paul, far from being annoyed that the Bereans should not simply take his word for it, was no doubt encouraged by their commitment to Scripture. He might have said, 'Yes, search the Scriptures; check it out and you will find that it all "fits"; all that I am telling you about Jesus – his life, death and resurrection – it is all there in the pages of the Old Testament Scriptures.'

The Bereans' attitude would have warmed Paul's heart. The same kind of response encouraged him when he preached the gospel for the first time in Thessalonica. When he later wrote to the Christians there he reminded them of their initial response to his preaching of the gospel:

> We thank God constantly for this, that when you received the word of God, which you heard from us, you accepted it not as the word of men, but as what it really is, the word of God, which is at work in you believers (1 Thess. 2:13).

It is a model of the Christian mindset – submitting to the authority of God's word and experiencing it shaping our minds and hearts.

> Speak, O Lord, as we come to You
> to receive the food of Your holy word;
> Take Your truth, plant it deep in us;
> shape and fashion us in Your likeness,
> That the light of Christ might be seen today
> in our acts of love and our deeds of faith.[1]

It is not that we are called to worship a book; it is wrong for critics to accuse evangelicals of bibliolatry. We worship the triune God, but when we ignore, set aside or turn away from his word, then we are opening ourselves up to deception and falsehood. When Calvin said in his comment on 2 Timothy 3:16 that we owe

[1] Hymn by Keith Getty & Stuart Townend, 2005.

to the Scripture the same reverence which we owe to God, he was not lapsing into the worship of a book, but recognising that since the Bible comes to us from the mouth of God (cf. Matt. 4:4) we must respect it, honour it, and obey it.

There is no greater threat to the health of the church than the side-lining of the Bible. The name of the Lord (his honour) and the word of the Lord are brought together in Psalm 138:2 and they are 'exalted above all things'.

In the early days of flying there was a heavy casualty toll in times of fog and mist. Many planes crashed, and one pilot was asked how he had survived flying in such conditions. His reply was that he relied on his instruments. Apparently pilots can experience an overwhelming sense in such circumstances that their instruments have malfunctioned and their readings must therefore be ignored. But that was the way of disaster. The better way was to rely on one's instruments. We err when we think we know better than God's word; better by far to rely on his truth. As Proverbs 3:5 says, 'Trust in the LORD with all your heart, and *do not lean on your own understanding*.'

This chapter has been concerned with the authority of the Bible. We honour the name of the Lord when we trust the word of the Lord. The two are brought together neatly in a paragraph of Jim Packer's in which he makes use of some words of Handley C. G. Moule (1841–1920), the evangelical Bishop of Durham:

> The Christian's use of the Bible must correspond with Christ's own use of the Bible. For, to quote some words of Bishop Handley Moule,
>
> 'He, in the days of his flesh, was the supreme Bible student, the supreme lover, employer, and expositor of the Bible. Look again at the fact as it stands out in the four Gospels. See "this same Jesus" as He upheld Himself and foiled the enemy with the Bible in the Temptation, as He opened His message with it at Nazareth, as He quoted its syllables twice over on the Cross. Walk to Emmaus with Him, and see Him spending the whole Easter afternoon upon the Bible. He had come that morning from the

> grave, conqueror of death, Lord of life, and He came as it were with the Bible in His hands.'
>
> He trampled upon many popular opinions of his day, where he thought they needed correction, but he did not trample upon the universal Jewish belief that the Bible was divine, the written word of God, declaring God's truth and imbued with God's authority. No, that belief he sanctioned and sanctified. And it is for us to treat the Bible as he did.[1]

All of the above considerations highlight the seriousness of the decisions taken by recent General Assemblies of the Church of Scotland. In the next chapter we will proceed to set these present controversies in their historical context, following the oft-quoted desire of Oliver Cromwell that his son should learn a little history.

[1] Packer, *Under God's Word*, 103-104.

6

A Little History

ROMANS 12:18 exhorts us to 'live peaceably with all'. Yet the full text is, 'If possible, so far as it depends on you, live peaceably with all.' The words 'if possible' remind us that there may be times when confrontation is unavoidable. The apostle who wrote these words was not shy of such confrontation when it was necessary, as illustrated in his famous disagreement with the apostle Peter. It must have been an highly-charged occasion when Paul, as he explained later, 'opposed him to his face' (Gal. 2:11). When gospel truth is at stake such confrontation is necessary.

Obviously, unity is a highly desirable goal. Jesus, after all, prayed that his people might be one (John 17:11), and Ephesians 4:3 says that Christians should be 'eager to maintain the unity of the Spirit in the bond of peace'. Indeed, Paul also exhorted us to 'Watch out for those who cause divisions and create obstacles contrary to the doctrine that you have been taught; avoid them. For such persons do not serve our Lord Christ' (Rom. 16:17-18).

If that is the biblical default position for God's people, is there any justification for secession? Divisions and secessions have been frequent features of the church's life, including the church in Scotland. The chart of divisions and reunions within Scottish Christianity is a very complicated one. It gives rise to some questions. Is secession ever the right thing? Is it justifiable to part company with a particular denomination of the church? And then there is the question we have raised previously: Does the responsibility for division lie with those who secede or with those whose unwise or unbiblical decisions have provoked the secession?

The argument of this book is that there *is* a time for secession. That time comes when the honour of God and his word is at stake. It is the time when a denomination persists in a rejection of God's truth, as in the days of Jeremiah. The prophet took no pleasure in proclaiming the Lord's message for his times; he spoke of it as 'a burning fire shut up in my bones, and I am weary with holding it in, and I cannot' (Jer. 20:9). His message was a message of coming judgment:

> Thus says the LORD: 'Stand by the roads, and look, and ask for the ancient paths, where the good way is, and walk in it, and find rest for your souls. But they said, "We will not walk in it." I set watchmen over you, saying, "Pay attention to the sound of the trumpet!" But they said, "We will not pay attention." Therefore hear, O nations, and know, O congregation, what will happen to them. Hear, O earth; behold I am bringing disaster upon this people, the fruit of their devices, because they have not paid attention to my words; and as for my law, they have rejected it"' (Jer. 6:16-19).

The Bible does not advocate unity at any cost, and in this chapter we will consider some historical instances of division, and the justification offered by those who, like evangelicals in the twenty-first century, have faced the critical question of when it is right to divide from people who reject or sit light to God's word.

It has been suggested that when Thomas Chalmers was born in 1780, 'It was about the deadest time in the history of the Church of Scotland since the Reformation.'[1] Today, even when we take account of the widespread nominalism that has often characterised membership of national churches and the falling-away of people who were members for social or formal reasons, the trends are worrying, and no one can be complacent or sanguine about them. At the same time it is hard to avoid the conclusion that the increasingly liberal ethos and direction of the denomination, with its low regard for Scripture, are taking a serious toll on its ability to fulfil

[1] Iain H. Murray, *A Scottish Christian Heritage* (Banner of Truth Trust, 2006), 79.

its own stated aim of ministering to the whole of Scotland or to survive as any kind of national church.

The 2013 Assembly was candidly told that the supply of ministerial candidates, particularly from evangelical congregations, had virtually dried up. Was this a surprise to anyone? If the Church of Scotland continues on its present liberal course, where does it think its next generation of ministers is going to come from? The more liberal the denomination, the less likely it is that potential future leaders will look to it; they will be more likely to consider service elsewhere.

There has been an increase in the number of evangelical ministries within the Church of Scotland in recent decades, but that increase has not translated into any significant change in the course of the denomination's life and character.[1] Many evangelicals have tried to maintain biblical truth within the structures of the Church of Scotland and there are also, of course, parishes and congregations which have seen great gospel effectiveness and advance, but the denomination as a whole is sadly in decline.

There is a phrase in a book that was given to me when I was a Sunday School pupil in a Church of Scotland congregation many years ago.[2] It was about some notable personalities in the story of Scottish Christianity and it described John Knox's task as the restoration of 'the purity and simplicity of Bible Christianity'. It is the Church of Scotland's relationship to 'Bible Christianity' that is the

[1] 'Membership has fallen by more than two-thirds in the past 40 years. ... Church historian, Professor Callum Brown of Dundee University, has charted the decline of the Kirk. He said: "Since 1963 the Church of Scotland has suffered a straight line graph of decline in its adherence. This decline has been sustained and at the moment is showing absolutely no sign of changing." In 1980 a report to the Kirk's Council of Ministry predicted the reduction in membership – and in 1997 the church suggested that if the decline in numbers continued, it would cease to exist by 2033.' Reeval Alderson, 'The Revolution that Created the Church of Scotland', BBC Scotland news report, 24 August 2010. http://www.bbc.co.uk/news/uk-scotland-11065965.

[2] Beatrice Mair Sawyer, *Seven Men Of The Kirk* (Church of Scotland Youth Committee, 1959), 35. The seven were Patrick Hamilton, George Wishart, John Knox, George Buchanan, Andrew Melville, Alexander Henderson, and William Carstares.

crux of the present problem, and as we look at certain historical episodes we shall see the truth of J. I. Packer's assertion: 'the dictum that the real schismatic is not the one who separates but the one who causes the separation has a long history'.[1] As the German theologian Wolfhart Pannenberg wrote (specifically in relation to the acceptance of homosexual practice as normal or good):

> Those who urge the church to change the norm of its teaching on this matter must know that they are promoting schism. If a church were to let itself be pushed to the point where it ceased to treat homosexual activity as a departure from the biblical norm, and recognized homosexual unions as a personal partnership of love equivalent to marriage, such a church would stand no longer on biblical ground but against the unequivocal witness of Scripture. A church that took this step would cease to be the one, holy, catholic, and apostolic church.[2]

Romans 16:17 bids us 'watch out for those who cause divisions and create obstacles contrary to the doctrine that you have been taught; avoid them'. Today 'those who cause divisions' are those who have persuaded the Church of Scotland to turn aside from the doctrine that it has been taught – the doctrine found in the Scriptures and recognised by the church throughout the ages.[3] It is now as it was long ago when King Ahab alleged that Elijah, with his call for uncompromising allegiance to the Lord God, was the 'troubler of Israel'. Elijah's response was, 'I have not troubled Israel, but you have, and your father's house, because you have abandoned the commandments of the LORD and followed the Baals' (1 Kings 18:17-18).

[1] J. I. Packer, *Taking God Seriously* (IVP, 2013), 101.

[2] *Revelation and Homosexual Experience* in *Christianity Today,* 11.11.96; available at http://www.christianitytoday.com/ct/1996/november11/6td035.html?start=3 (accessed 5.12.14)

[3] Cf. the Presbyterian Church of Australia, which in 1977 refused to join the ecumenical Uniting Church. One minister said on behalf of those who remained outside the union, 'We protest before the great God, Searcher of all hearts, that we and all who adhere to us, are not responsible for this schism in the Church or for any consequence which may flow from this enforced separation.' C. R. Thomas, *The Crisis of '77* (PTC Media, 2004), 23.

With such considerations in mind, we can set the present departure of many from the Church of Scotland in a historical context, which we shall illustrate by reference to the sixteenth-century Reformation, the nineteenth-century Disruption in Scotland, the 'Fundamentalist' controversies in early twentieth-century America, and the controversy surrounding the call of Martyn Lloyd-Jones for evangelical separation in the mid-twentieth century.

The Reformation

As a loyal Augustinian monk, Martin Luther tried hard to fit in with the Church's life. Even when he nailed his famous ninety-five theses to the door of the Castle Church in Wittenberg on the last day of October 1517, he was hoping for a reformation with a small 'r' rather than the cataclysmic revolution that resulted in 'The Reformation'. But in 1521 he was summoned to appear before the Diet of Worms, convened by Charles V, the Holy Roman Emperor, to give an account of himself – and, from the point of view of the Papacy, to retract the newfangled doctrines found in his books. Luther, however, was not for turning: his conscience was bound to the word of God and, unless it could be shown from Scripture that he had taught false doctrine, he would not recant.

The Reformation which he reluctantly initiated was nothing if not a rediscovery of the authority and power of the Scriptures, the written word of God.

The centrality of the word of God is also seen in the life of the Swiss Reformer, Ulrich Zwingli. When he came to realise that he had read and studied many commentaries on the Bible but had not read the actual Bible, he took the revolutionary step of studying the Book itself. 'At the time, to go straight to the Bible and seek to understand it was considered dangerously subversive. Without the pope's guidance, people could make the Bible say anything. Worse, it implied that the pope was not God's appointed interpreter of Scripture. It was a slippery slope to schism, to walking away from the embrace of Mother Church.'[1]

[1] Michael Reeves, *The Unquenchable Flame* (IVP, 2009), 62.

This 'walking away' from Mother Church, however, was a necessary but reluctant step for the reformers, just as it has been for many members of the Church of Scotland in recent years. In an interesting comment, Rev. Ivor MacDonald has suggested that it is illogical to regard one denomination (in this case the Church of Scotland) as '*the* church' and to declare that it is an act of schism to part from that denomination when in truth that denomination itself came into being when its founders departed from another church which was understood to have departed from the word of God.

Secession

Scotland has had a long succession of secessions. The Revolution Settlement of 1688 had re-established Presbyterianism in Scotland and abolished the system of patronage under which congregations were expected to accept ministers placed in post by local landowners.[1] But in 1712 Parliament restored it, and this caused much controversy for many years; the root cause of much disruption was this issue: Should a congregation not have the right to call the minister of its choice rather than having someone 'foisted' upon it?

Thomas Gillespie was minister of Carnock (near Dunfermline) from 1741 to 1752. In 1752 the General Assembly ordered the Presbytery of Dunfermline to induct to the charge of Inverkeithing a minister who was the presentee of the patron. The Inverkeithing parishioners were opposed to this, and the Presbytery, of which Gillespie was a member, held to the view that no Church Court has the right to 'intrude' a minister on a congregation against its will.

[1] By way of illustration of patronage: Kenneth Roxburgh refers to figures from later (1769) when the rights of patronage stood as follows: 334 in the hands of the Crown; 309 in the hands of the nobility; 233 in the hands of landed gentry; 45 in the hands of burghs, and 2 in burghs of barony; 3 in the hands of heritors and elders. K. Roxburgh, *Thomas Gillespie and the Origins of the Relief Church in 18th Century Scotland.*

At that time the Assembly would often over-ride the will of Presbyteries and appoint inductions to be carried out by individuals unconnected with the Presbytery ('riding committees'), men who were prepared to obey instructions even in the teeth of local protests. Over fifty ministers were so inducted. Interestingly, an appendix to the Joint Report to the 2015 General Assembly of the Legal Questions Committee and the Theological Forum found it necessary to say, 'If required, a Presbytery shall invite one or more members of one or more other Presbyteries to associate with the Presbytery for the purpose of effecting an ordination, induction or introduction.'

In 1752 the Assembly decided to force Presbyteries to conduct inductions and singled out Thomas Gillespie, who was one of six objectors to the Inverkeithing induction, in order to make an example of him. 'His supporters secured a meeting-house in Dunfermline, which became the first home of the new congregation, where Gillespie continued to minister until his death'[1] (in 1774). Gillespie and two other ministers formed themselves into a presbytery – for 'the relief of Christians oppressed in their Christian privileges'. By the time when this Relief Church joined with the United Secession Church in 1847, it had 136 congregations. Gillespie's ideals survived and in many ways triumphed, in that the eighty-six-year history of the Relief Church was one of the factors which brought into modern times the right of congregations to call their own ministers.

The Disruption

The issue of patronage continued to be a problem. To many it was clearly wrong that landowners, whether they were committed believers or not, should have the power of placing ministers in congregations.

It can also be said that behind the particular issue lay the divide between evangelicals and liberals (or moderates, as they were often

[1] http://gillespiechurch.org/history2.html.

called). Towards the end of the eighteenth century, evangelicals represented a significant 'wing' within the Church of Scotland, although the General Assembly was largely controlled by moderates. However, by 1834, evangelicals led by Thomas Chalmers had increased in strength and, as well as initiating a vigorous church extension campaign, they managed to persuade the Assembly to pass the Veto Act which gave heads of households the right to block the appointment of a patron's nominee for a vacant parish. The Act stated, 'It is a fundamental law of this Church that no pastor shall be intruded on any congregation contrary to the will of the people.'

This marked the start of the Ten Years' Conflict and it was not long before the Veto Act was challenged. In 1834 in Auchterarder the land-owner presented a candidate for the vacant pulpit. Three people signed the call and 287 voted against. The General Assembly accordingly instructed the Presbytery to reject the candidate, but when the candidate appealed to the (civil) Court of Session, the Court upheld the appeal and ruled that the Church had acted beyond its powers. The President of the Court said, 'The Parliament is the temporal head of the Church, from whose Acts, and from whose Acts alone, it exists as a National Church, and from which it derives its powers.'[1] This was a clear challenge to the self-understanding of the Church as subservient to Christ alone.

Then in 1837 the minister at Marnoch in Aberdeenshire died and the patron nominated a minister who was known to be a heavy drinker – the local innkeeper was the only person to sign the call! Two hundred and sixty-one people signed the veto against him but the local Presbytery resolved to proceed with the ordination – even when snowballs were thrown at them! The local people protested and insisted that a congregation should be able to call its own minister. Eventually the Presbytery inducted the man (though seven ministers were suspended by the Assembly for proceeding with the induction) and some members decided to break away and to form a new congregation.

[9] Quoted by R. Burrows, *Signposts From the Past* (Lulu, 2013), 163.

'In 1838 ... the Court of Session, the highest civil court in Scotland, declared the Church's Veto Act to be an illegal encroachment on the property rights of patrons – a decision upheld by the House of Lords the following year.'[1] Parliament rejected all appeals and the stage was set for the dramatic events of 18 May 1843 when a mass exodus took place from that year's General Assembly in St Andrew's Church in George Street, Edinburgh. Ministers and elders marched down the hill to Tanfield Hall (a plaque now marks the site in the Canonmills district) where they formed themselves into the Free Church of Scotland under the Moderatorship of Thomas Chalmers.

The Act of Separation was signed by 474 ministers (almost 40% of ministers then serving). 'They surrendered stipends worth approximately £100,000 per annum, along with their churches, manses and social status, all for an uncertain future.'[2]

These ministers were joined by about half the membership of the Church of Scotland. Many people were prepared to generously and sacrificially support the new denomination. In the tax year 1844–45 more than £334,000 was collected, which included money from middle- and upper-class people but also from many of the tenant farmers who resented the power of the landowners and strove for economic independence.[3]

In the post-Disruption period the Free Church erected 500 church buildings in its first year and within five years had constructed 500 parish schools, 400 manses, and 730 church buildings. It also established three divinity colleges and took on the support of overseas missionary work (all but one of the Church of Scotland's missionaries joined the Free Church). 'It collected money at the rate of a thousand pounds a day, and thereby taught Scotsmen a new conception of liberality.'[4]

[1] Stewart J. Brown in *Disruption to Diversity: Edinburgh Divinity 1846–1996*, D. F. Wright & G. D. Badcock, eds. (T & T Clark, 1996), 32.

[2] Stewart J Brown, *Scotland in the Age of the Disruption* (Edinburgh University Press, 1993), 21.

[3] *Ibid.*, 23.

[4] John Buchan, *The Kirk in Scotland* (Labarum Publications, 1985), 79.

All of this activity took place against a background of opposition and all manner of attempts were made to frustrate and hinder it. This has also been a feature of the recent controversies: the 'establishment' has put obstacles in the way of seceders from the Church of Scotland, particularly in parishes where committed members have raised and spent very large sums of money in maintaining and enhancing church buildings.

Many nineteenth-century landowners sought to make things as difficult as possible for the new denomination. They would often refuse congregations ground on which to build churches or manses. John Fowler has incidentally given two interesting pictures of the ingenuity sometimes provoked by such measures.

- The floating church at Ardnamurchan became something of a *cause célèbre*. It was a barge which could accommodate 600 worshippers. A gauge at the bow showed that for every hundred people on board the boat sank an inch so that a visiting preacher who attracted a large congregation could be given the great accolade of having made the church sink lower than ever before!

- 'Tents were another solution. Even as the Disruption Assembly met, a smart London entrepreneur had arrived in Edinburgh, offering tents for sale ... tents sprang up all over the country. To his surprise and delight, the minister at Blairgowrie, north of Dundee, returned from the Assembly to find a large tent pitched on ground adjoining the glebe. It seated a thousand on close-packed benches.'[1]

Despite opposition, however, the Free Church pressed ahead, under the inspiring leadership of a man who has been described as 'the uncrowned king of Scotland',[2] a sentiment echoed by Hugh Miller in his description of Chalmers' funeral in 1847, when it was estimated that 100,000 people lined the streets of Edinburgh as the cortège made its way to the Grange Cemetery. Chalmers was

[1] J. Fowler, *Mr Hill's Big Picture* (Saint Andrew Press, 2006), 134.
[2] *Ibid.*, 4.

not interested in any kind of empire-building; his motivation was 'the Christian good of the people of Scotland'. This was one of his famous sayings: 'Who cares about the Free Church compared with the Christian good of the people of Scotland?'

Patronage was a big subject but, as suggested above, the cleavage between liberalism and evangelicalism was the underlying issue, just as it can be said today that, although the presenting issue is the appointment of practising homosexuals as ministers, behind and underneath that lies the deeper issue of radically different attitudes to the Bible.

Patronage was abolished in 1874, and in 1900, as already noted, most of the Free Church united with the United Presbyterian Church to form the United Free Church, most of which reunited with the Church of Scotland in 1929. Some Free Church congregations did not enter the Reunion and there are currently over 100 Free Church congregations in Scotland and also a Theological Seminary in Edinburgh.

In my book *Believe It or Not* I considered the matter of whether such division calls into question the message of Christianity:

> There may be no excuse for disunity, but at least we should remember that when we are talking about 'religious' issues, we are talking about issues on which people feel very deeply. It is not on a level with whether you are interested in football, fashion or philately. People may become passionately committed to such pastimes, but few even of the most enthusiastic devotees would claim that their interests are matters of life and death. It doesn't really matter whether I support a particular football team, favour a particular style in fashion or put everything into stamp-collecting. But when it comes to the issues which lie at the heart of 'religion', we are talking about matters of the greatest importance. Christians believe that the questions involved in our response to Jesus Christ are crucial for everyone – both for their immediate fulfilment in this life and for their eternal well-being. The very fact that Christians take such issues so seriously means that differences will not seem trivial but very important.[1]

[1] David J. Randall, *Believe It or Not* (Rutherford House, 2000), 113-114.

Fundamentalism

Of course, it is not only Scotland that has been affected by such issues. In the United States, when J. Gresham Machen (1881–1937) was faced with the question of how to respond to liberalism, his frankly-expressed contrast was not between liberal Christianity and evangelical Christianity but between (in terms of the title of one of his books) *Christianity & Liberalism*.

He made the point emphasised above when he wrote,

> In the sphere of religion, as in other spheres, the things about which men are agreed are apt to be the things that are least worth holding; the really important things are the things about which men will fight.[1]

And, he wrote, again with (from an evangelical perspective) a refreshing candour,

> The chief modern rival of Christianity is 'liberalism.' An examination of the teachings of liberalism in comparison with those of Christianity will show that at every point the two movements are in direct opposition.[2]

That was in the early part of the twentieth century; in this early part of the twenty-first century, our situation could be described in similar terms. For a long time there have been two different religions operating within the Church of Scotland. The middle ground between the two was once large, and was occupied by people who gave nominal consent to the creeds and confessions and to the standards of Christian morality but whose commitment to the gospel was less than wholehearted. Today that middle ground is fast disappearing. To say such things is not to be belligerent or intolerant; it is simply facing up to facts.

No human being can discern with absolute certainty who are true Christians and who are not; we may distinguish between

[1] *Christianity & Liberalism* (1923; Eerdmans, 2009), 1-2.

[2] *Ibid.*, 45. Machen goes on to illustrate this thesis in consideration of successive subjects: God and Man, the Bible, Christ, Salvation and the Church.

the visible and the invisible church,[1] but it is the Lord alone who knows the hearts of human beings (1 Sam. 16:7; Psa. 139:1); only he knows who truly belong to him (2 Tim. 2:19). The visible church will always be a mixed company, and there must be a way in for enquirers – people who want to know more before committing themselves to Christ. The fellowship and public life of churches should be such that people can indeed investigate, but *membership* must involve a profession of faith and commitment to discipleship. Clearly it is possible for people to profess such commitment in a purely formal way, so that the church ends up with some people whose membership is merely nominal. A *Life & Work* article has even suggested that congregations and ministers should not assert that people's belonging 'depends on their ability to tick certain boxes of belief ... Don't insist on belief before belonging – faith comes with belonging.'[2] The idea that people should be admitted to membership without actually believing in God is an evangelistic strategy unknown to the apostolic church of the New Testament.

If there ought to be some requirement for church membership, the same ought to apply to those who preach and teach. Indeed, we may recall the sobering word of the apostle James, 'Not many of you should become teachers, my brothers, for you know that we who teach will be judged with greater strictness' (James 3:1). All of us are 'unworthy servants' (Luke 17:10), but the church ought not to ordain people who sit loose to the teaching of God's word in Scripture. It is the church's responsibility to ensure that its ministers and leaders are people who actually believe in Christianity! They are to be people who exercise the twin qualities 'fidelity to the Word of God and care for the people of God'.[3]

[1] Cf. 'The catholick church hath been sometimes more, sometimes less visible. And particular churches, which are members thereof, are more or less pure, according as the doctrine of the gospel is taught and embraced, ordinances administered, and publick worship performed more or less purely in them. ... The purest churches under heaven are subject both to mixture and error.' Westminster Confession of Faith, XXV.4, 5.

[2] J. Chalmers, article in *Life & Work*, August 2014.

[3] Foreword by Alec Motyer in Ian Barclay, *He is Everything to Me* (CPAS

Returning to the fundamentalist controversies in the United States, Gresham Machen was a Presbyterian minister who taught New Testament at Princeton Theological Seminary. After the death of his colleague B. B. Warfield, he became a leading representative of the old Princeton Theology, and when he came to believe that the Seminary was moving in a liberal direction, he resigned and became one of the founders of Westminster Theological Seminary in Philadelphia.

There he served as President and Professor of New Testament from 1929 to 1937. He also became one of the founders and leaders of the Orthodox Presbyterian Church – 'founded in 1936 after a long struggle within the Presbyterian Church in the USA between theological conservatives who sought to conform the denomination to its doctrinal constitution, the Westminster Confession of Faith, and their opponents who were willing to tolerate theological "modernism".'[1]

On the rationale of separation, Machen wrote,

> We are not dealing here with delicate personal questions; we are not presuming to say whether such and such an individual man is a Christian or not. God only can decide such questions; no man can say with assurance whether the attitude of certain individual 'liberals' toward Christ is saving faith or not. But one thing is perfectly plain – whether or not liberals are Christians, it is at any rate perfectly clear that liberalism is not Christianity. And that being the case, it is highly undesirable that liberalism and Christianity should continue to be propagated within the bounds of the same organization. A separation between the two parties in the Church is the crying need of the hour.[2]

Machen made the point that it is really liberals who should leave an orthodox church. Honesty should lead those to depart who no longer believe the fundamental doctrines of the church. That at least would be laudable integrity. When, however, as in

---

Falcon Books, 1972), 7.

[1] Article by G. Marsden in *The New International Dictionary of the Christian Church* (Zondervan, 1974), 735.

[2] Machen, *Christianity & Liberalism*, 135-36.

the case of the Church of Scotland now, liberalism is bedded in and even applauded, many evangelical people have felt compelled to depart. By its decision to approve the induction of persons in active homosexual relationships, the Church has openly declared its abandonment of the Bible as its supreme rule of faith and life. This has been done deliberately and repeatedly over the years, despite cogent and gracious argument from a biblical standpoint and despite all warnings about the consequences of such a decision.

This sad departure from Scripture necessitates a sad departure from the denomination.

Lloyd-Jones / John Stott

It is sometimes claimed that evangelicals, while standing firmly against liberalism in the church, ought to remain within liberal or mixed denominations in order to contend there for orthodoxy and to seek to reclaim their denomination. John Stott famously resisted a call by Martyn Lloyd-Jones for evangelical secession. In Scotland, it is claimed that the influential evangelical leader William Still would have resisted the departure of evangelicals from the Church of Scotland and would have advocated a policy of 'quiet infiltration' of the ranks of liberalism. Mr Still's position was discussed in chapter 3, so we now turn to one of the most ecclesiastically significant dates of the twentieth century – 18 October 1966.

The setting was the National Assembly of Evangelicals at Methodist Central Hall, Westminster. The chairman was Dr John Stott and the speaker was Dr Martyn Lloyd-Jones. Lloyd-Jones issued a stirring call for evangelical unity, claiming that evangelicals were weak and ineffective when scattered about in mixed denominations ('broad churches'), whether Anglican, Presbyterian, Congregationalist, or whatever. He alleged that evangelical disunity was sinful and proclaimed 'that evangelicals had no right to ask God's blessing on churches which denied the essentials of the faith, but if they stood together they could expect the Holy Spirit to fall in "mighty revival and re-awakening"'.[1]

We are told that the atmosphere was electric as chairman John Stott rose to close the meeting and urged people not to make precipitate decisions after Dr Lloyd-Jones' address. He expressed the view that history was against the Doctor, that others had tried to do the same thing, and that in Scripture the remnant was within the church.

Although Lloyd-Jones had not actually talked of secession,[2] the following year he wrote a letter to his own congregation in which he appealed 'to all truly Evangelical people in all the denominations to come together and to form local independent Evangelical churches which should be in a loose fellowship together in order that the world might hear and see a living witness to the truth of the Gospel'.[3] It is ironic that a National Assembly of Evangelicals which was meant to foster evangelical unity should end up being the focus of increasing disunity.

A letter in the *Church of England Newspaper* expressed the reaction of stayers (perhaps in unusually vigorous language):

> Secede? How on earth was the Reformation won? By writing cry-baby letters, as some do, to Evangelical newspapers threatening to run out if this or that isn't prevented? The enemies of Christ would only laugh! ... As one of the determined stay-putters, I can only assert, 'Let 'em all come!' Certainly we could all retire, if we wished, to a large live Church, but cosy hothouse atmospheres

[1] Andrew Atherstone & D. Ceri Jones, *Engaging with Martyn Lloyd-Jones* (Apollos, IVP, 2011), 270-71.

[2] Iain H. Murray, who was Assistant to Martyn Lloyd-Jones at Westminster Chapel from 1956 to 1959, has set Lloyd-Jones' views in the context of the twentieth-century ecumenical movement, particularly in its hope for an eventual union with the Roman Catholic Church. 'Because of the success of ecumenical thinking, with its call to end denominational divisions and to seek "one church", there was a new question before evangelicals; it was whether they would continue within *that* church.' *Evangelicalism Divided* (Banner of Truth Trust, 2000), 283.

[3] Westminster Chapel Archives, 1 January 1967; quoted in *Engaging with Martyn Lloyd-Jones*, 273.

never breed saints. Saints are tough. Let those who are fight-shy get out. The Church will be richer without them![1]

A different emphasis was expressed jointly by Alan Stibbs, Oliver Barclay, and Nigel Sylvester (respectively ex Vice-Principal of Oak Hill Theological College, General Secretary of IVF, and General Secretary of Scripture Union):

> Most evangelical Anglican clergy are now so committed to the Church of England that they are unwilling to fix certain points beyond which they cannot go. They give the impression that they would stay in however far its official formularies and structures were altered ... Denominational loyalties, which are without clear biblical warrant, seem to take precedence over questions of truth.[2]

This matches the expressed views not only of Church of Scotland liberals, who refer to compromise decisions as good for the peace and unity of the church, but also of some evangelical stayers who seem determined to remain within the Church no matter how far it strays from scriptural truth.

The debate rumbled on within the Church of England with the gulf widening following the National Evangelical Anglican Congress at Keele in April 1967. More than a dozen evangelical ministers seceded from the Church of England in the decade after Keele.[3]

Later, in 1977, when John Stott was President of the Evangelical Alliance, he said in a speech:

> ... some evangelicals, like myself, believe it is the will of God to remain in a church that is sometimes called a 'mixed denomination'. At least until it becomes apostate and ceases to be a church, we believe it is our duty to remain in it and bear witness to the truth as we have been given to understand it.[4]

[1] *Engaging with Martyn Lloyd-Jones*, 275.

[2] Memorandum, *Evangelical Witness and Unity*, December 1970, quoted in *Ibid.*, 290.

[3] *Engaging with Martyn Lloyd-Jones*, 282.

[4] Quoted in: Timothy Dudley-Smith, *John Stott: A Global Ministry* (IVP, 2001), 70.

It is interesting to add to all of this John Stott's own comment, made during a visit in 1978 to Martyn Lloyd-Jones. When Lloyd-Jones asked the straight question, 'Would you ever leave the Church of England?', Stott's frank response was, 'Yes indeed, I could envisage such a situation, if the Church itself compromised officially one of the central doctrines of the faith. I'm not committed to the Church of England irrevocably.'[1]

In a later essay, *Why I am still a Member of the Church of England*, published in 2007,[2] Stott stated, 'There could be an extreme situation ... when the only course would be to secede' (the example he gave was an official repudiation of the incarnation). The obvious question is: what else would count as 'an extreme situation'? Would rejection of the binding authority of Scripture be such a situation? This has been the issue facing many people in Scotland in light of the recent developments described above in chapter 2. It is all too easy to ignore such questions and hope that they will go away, but they will not.

The cover blurb for Stott's *The Authentic Jesus* states that the book was written in response to much-publicised statements from some churchmen in which they expressed doubt about the virgin birth and the bodily resurrection of our Lord. Similar things have happened in Scotland, and when people ask why evangelicals should leave a denomination now when they have not done so in light of such expressions of unbelief, the answer is that while it may be bad when such views are expressed by individuals, it is much worse when the rejection of Scripture becomes the official position of a denomination. Nothing is to be gained from sweeping such issues under the carpet.

Towards the end of *The Authentic Jesus*, John Stott wrote:

> Nowadays all kinds of controversy are distasteful, and none more so than religious controversy. Yet to shrink from it is characteristic

[1] *Ibid.*, 174. It is interesting to note the high esteem in which John Stott held Martyn Lloyd-Jones. In an obituary prepared for *The Times* Stott described his friend as the 'most powerful and persuasive voice in Britain for some thirty years'. J. I. Packer also referred to him as 'The greatest man I have ever known.'

[2] One of three historical appendices to his *The Living Church* (IVP, 2007), 172.

> of the age of uncertainty in which we are living, not of Jesus Christ and his apostles; they contended vigorously for what they believed to be the truth ... It is more healthy and more honest to bring our disagreements out into the open.[1]

Before returning to the situation in Scotland, we may refer to another well-known Anglican, J. I. Packer. He opposed the view of Martyn Lloyd-Jones in 1966 and later controversially co-authored *Growing into Union* with two Anglo-Catholics. Since 1979 he has lived in Vancouver and is associated with St John's Vancouver Anglican Church, which in February 2008 voted to leave the Anglican Church of Canada over the issue of same-sex blessings. In April of that year Packer handed in his licence to his bishop.[2]

When in 2002 the Synod of the Anglican Diocese of New Westminster authorized its bishop to produce a service for blessing same-sex unions, a number of synod members walked out in protest. One of them was Dr Packer and, in an article in *Christianity Today*, he explained 'Why I Walked.' His answer gives food for thought for all who face the issue of whether to stay or leave a denomination.

> Why did I walk out with the others? Because this decision, taken in its context, falsifies the gospel of Christ, abandons the authority of Scripture, jeopardizes the salvation of fellow human beings, and betrays the church in its God-appointed role as the bastion and bulwark of divine truth.

Packer writes with his characteristic lucidity and I recommend following the URL in the footnote[3] to read his comments. Packer has elsewhere written:

> A much-publicized Episcopal decision in Canada to bless same-sex unions as if they were marriages, as well as the consecrating in the United States of a diocesan bishop who unashamedly lives in such a union, has convulsed global Anglicanism in the way that

[1] *The Authentic Jesus* (Marshall Morgan and Scott, 1985), 85.

[2] http://en.wikipedia.org/wiki/J._I._Packer (accessed 22.8.14).

[3] http://www.christianitytoday.com/ct/2003/january/6.46.html?paging=off (accessed 22.8.14).

pebbles thrown into a pond send ripples over the entire surface of the water.[1]

In brief, he begins by making certain points about Paul's warning in 1 Corinthians 6:9-11 concerning people who 'will not inherit the kingdom of God'. They include sexually immoral people, idolaters and men who practise homosexuality as well as thieves, the greedy and swindlers. The life-changing power of the gospel is reflected in the following words, 'And such were some of you. But you were washed, you were sanctified, you were justified in the name of the Lord Jesus Christ and by the Spirit of our God.'

Packer asks and answers four questions about Paul's list:

> 1. What is Paul talking about in this vice list? Answer: Lifestyles, regular behaviour patterns, habits of mind and action. He has in view not single lapses followed by repentance, forgiveness, and greater watchfulness (with God's help) against recurrence, but ways of life in which some of his readers were set, believing that for Christians there was no harm in them.
>
> 2. What is Paul saying about these habits? Answer: They are ways of sin that, if not repented of and forsaken, will keep people out of God's kingdom of salvation ...
>
> 3. What is Paul saying about homosexuality? Answer: Those who claim to be Christ's should avoid the practice of same-sex physical connection for orgasm, on the model of heterosexual intercourse ... [H]e is not speaking of inclinations, only of behaviour ...
>
> 4. What is Paul saying about the gospel? Answer: Those who, as lost sinners, cast themselves in genuine faith on Christ and so receive the Holy Spirit, as all Christians do (see Gal. 3:2), find transformation ...

Packer's 'Why I Walked' article also includes the reminder, 'At issue here is a Grand Canyon-wide difference about the nature of the Bible and the way it conveys God's message to modern readers.'

[1] *Taking God Seriously* (IVP, 2013), 17.

This points us back again to the heart of the matter before the Church of Scotland. It is all too easy for critics to make allegations about intolerance and so-called 'homophobia' but we come back to the fact that the underlying issue is not homosexual practice as such but the Church's attitude to God's revealed truth in Scripture. 'We cannot have the Jesus of the Bible without also having the Bible of Jesus.'[1]

* * *

In this chapter we have referred in broad outline to some historical highlights in relation to the issue of secession, stopping off at the Reformation in Europe, the Secessions and Disruption in Scotland, the Fundamentalist controversies in the United States, the Lloyd-Jones/John Stott dispute in England and J. I. Packer's experience in Canada. It leaves us with the big question: *What to do?*

[1] Zaspel, *The Theology of B. B. Warfield*, 51.

7
What Now?

IN the introductory chapter of this book I referred to a DVD which was commissioned for Kirk Session and Presbytery meetings by the Special Commission appointed by the General Assembly of 2009. I was invited to represent the 'traditionalist' view and I recall that the minister who represented the revisionist view posed a revealing question. He asked: If we go down that road (refusing to induct practising homosexual people as ministers), how will that look in the eyes of our society?

Such a comment invites a two-fold response. In the first place, we may well ask why anyone would respect a church that changes its standards according to the direction in which the current social wind is blowing. It is not only double-minded *individuals* who are unstable in all their ways (James 1:8), but double-minded *churches* also. However much it may seem sometimes that the (non-Christian) world is happy to give a place at the table to a vacillating church that bends with every wind (Matt. 11:7), surely we could neither expect nor deserve anything but contempt if we chop and change according to current social trends.

The other response, which is the orthodox response of the church of all the ages, reminds us that the big issue here is not 'political' but 'theological'; our concern is not what the world thinks of us but what God thinks of us. 'Truth out of vogue is truth still.'[1]

It is of course true that the church is called to commend the gospel to the wider society. The apostle Paul writes to Titus about the

[1] Zaspel, *The Theology of B. B. Warfield*, 556.

need for Christians to live in such a way as to 'adorn the doctrine of God our Saviour in all things'; the NIV translates it, 'so that in every way they will make the teaching about God our Saviour attractive' (Titus 2:10). The Bible has many admonitions of this kind; we are to do our utmost to commend the faith we hold by the lives we live and the witness we bear before a watching world. The apostle Paul even spoke about becoming 'all things to all people, that by all means I might save some. I do it all for the sake of the gospel' (1 Cor. 9:22-23).

However, there is a difference between endeavouring to be culturally relevant and allowing the culture to shape and mould our attitudes, or between being seeker-sensitive and seeker-driven. We are not called to commend the gospel by making it something other than it is, or by toning down its demands in order to make it more attractive to unbelievers. The Christian is a follower of One who was 'despised and rejected by men' (Isa. 53:3) and the servant should not expect better treatment than his Master (John 15:20). Christianity is not designed to make churches or Christians popular. Sometimes the cost of gaining a place at the world's table is simply too high. Gospel faithfulness calls for resistance to the seductive voices that offer us acceptance and even power so long as we do not say or do certain things the world dislikes. It is the temptation to 'fit in' – when, of course, the call of Scripture is, 'Do not be conformed to this world, but be transformed by the renewal of your mind, that by testing you may discern what is the will of God, what is good and acceptable and perfect' (Rom. 12:2).

Sometimes, especially if a numerical decline has taken place, there is the temptation to think that our stance or our patterns of worship or styles of church life 'are not working' and therefore we need to change. It may sometimes be so, of course, and clearly we are not bound to the *methods* of yesteryear. Change may be called for in certain regards, but we have no mandate to contradict or to sit loose to the *truth* that God has revealed to us.

The phrase we have quoted from Titus 2 (about living lives that will be attractive advertisements of the faith we profess) is found in a chapter that begins with the instruction, 'Teach what accords with sound doctrine' (Titus 2:1), and immediately after the verse, the apostle goes on to say: 'For the grace of God has appeared, bringing salvation for all people, training us to renounce ungodliness and worldly passions, and to live self-controlled, upright, and godly lives in the present age, waiting for our blessed hope, the appearing of the glory of our great God and Saviour Jesus Christ, who gave himself for us to redeem us from all lawlessness and to purify for himself a people for his own possession who are zealous for good works' (Titus 2:11-14).

Commenting on the words of Paul about becoming all things to all people in hope of winning some, the late James S. Stewart wrote:

> The greatest drag on Christianity today, the most serious menace to the church's mission, is not the secularism without, it is the reduced Christianity within: the religious generalities and innocuous platitudes of a pallid, anaemic Christianity which is simply (in the language of arithmeticians) the 'highest common factor' of half a dozen different religions. ... Did not Paul himself say, 'I am become all things to all men, that I might by all means save some'? Yes, indeed: but not at the self-defeating cost of changing Christianity into something else, not at the cost of soft-pedalling the historical-supernatural elements without which Christianity does not exist, or of dissolving the divine intolerance of the faith in a morass of religious relativism.[1]

These words were written over sixty years ago, but they are more relevant than ever. To ask what any decision would look like in the eyes of our society may not be unimportant, but it is by no means the main thing. The main thing about the church's life in every area must be: How does it look (not in the eyes of the world but) in the eyes of God? This God is not some deity of our own fashioning who would never 'say boo to a goose', but he is the living God who exists outside of us, the eternal triune God whom

[1] J. S. Stewart, *A Faith to Proclaim* (Hodder & Stoughton, 1953), 31-32.

we would not know at all if it were not that he has made himself known to us.

> The idea that Christianity stands chiefly in danger from the forces of materialism, or from secular philosophy, or from pagan religions, is not the teaching of the New Testament. The greatest danger comes rather from temptations within ... a large part of the preservation and defence of the church lies in resolute resistance to falsehood and in forthright teaching of the truth.[1]

At different times the crunch may come in connection with different issues. At present the issue is the question of the ordination of practising homosexuals to the ministry. Are we to ask how the Church's decisions will look in the eyes of society? Should we not rather be asking how the Church's decisions will look in the eyes of God? The important question is: Are we being faithful to what he has revealed?

What does the New Testament say?

- 'See to it that no one takes you captive by philosophy and empty deceit, according to human tradition, according to the elemental spirits of the world, and not according to Christ' (Col. 2:8).

- 'The time is coming when people will not endure sound teaching, but having itching ears they will accumulate for themselves teachers to suit their own passions' (2 Tim. 4:3).

- 'Do not believe every spirit, but test the spirits to see whether they are from God, for many false prophets have gone out into the world' (1 John 4:1).

- 'Contend for the faith that was once for all delivered to the saints' (Jude 3).

- 'I have a few things against you: you have some there who hold the teaching of Balaam, who taught Balak to put a stumbling block before the sons of Israel, so that they might eat food sacrificed to

[1] Murray, *Evangelicalism Divided*, 259.

idols and practise sexual immorality. ... Therefore, repent. If not, I will come to you soon and war against them with the sword of my mouth.' (Rev. 2:14-16).

- 'If anyone takes away from the words of the book of this prophecy, God will take away his share in the tree of life and in the holy city' (Rev. 22:19).

Among evangelicals there is not really any disagreement about the issue at stake in the recent controversy within the Church of Scotland. The issue at stake is the place and authority of the Bible in the Church. It is in connection with a proper response to the crisis that disagreement has arisen, with some believing that they should remain within the Church of Scotland with the aim of bringing it back to its proper foundations, while others have concluded that 'the game is up' and it is time for a sad departure.

In such a time there must be an attitude of respect and the avoidance of acrimony. To disagree without being disagreeable is a worthy ambition in such situations. Francis Schaeffer, referring to the American controversies in the 1930s (which led Gresham Machen and others to leave Princeton and found Westminster Theological Seminary), looked back with the reflection:

> We must show forth the love of God to those with whom we differ. Thirty-five years ago in the Presbyterian crisis in the United States, we forgot that. We did not speak with love about those with whom we differed, and we have been paying a high price for it ever since.[1]

This book has sought to provide a record of recent events and decisions which have led many (ministers, elders, and members) to depart from the Church of Scotland. We are presently in a time of transition and it is difficult at this juncture to see the pattern of church and denominational life that is going to emerge from the

[1] In *The Church Before the Watching World*, as quoted by Murray in *Evangelicalism Divided*, 310.

present turmoil; as the Chinese proverb says, it is hard to prophesy – especially about the future.

Unfortunately those who have made a sad departure from the Church of Scotland have not been able to act together in a concerted way, and different decisions have been made and continue to be made. The present situation is not like that of the Disruption of 1843,[1] even though it concerns a more fundamental issue than that which triggered the events of that year. The historian and politician Lord Macaulay (1800–59) expressed the view that it was from the Patronage Act of 1712 that 'undoubtedly flowed every secession and schism that has taken place in the Church of Scotland'.[2] That may have been true of the eighteenth- and nineteenth-century schisms, but in the twenty-first century Church of Scotland an even more fundamental matter is the focus of division, namely the Church's attitude to the word of God.

Why then has there not been a more united response from Bible-believing evangelicals? In previous pages we have considered reasons given by some evangelicals for not leaving the denomination. Would things have been different if there had been a 'charismatic' leader (a modern-day Chalmers, let us say), a high-profile statesmanlike leader. Could that have led to a more united response? Who can say? But it seems that the ethos of our times does not really lend itself to the emergence of 'statesmen' in the way of previous generations (either in the church or in society at large).

The largest single movement has been towards the Free Church of Scotland. This might be regarded as the most natural recourse, and the Free Church's 2010 decision regarding hymnody probably played a significant part in preparing the way[3]. At a special

[1] C. H. Spurgeon wrote regarding the downgrading of the authority of Scripture, 'The question in debate at the Disruption was secondary compared with that which is now at issue.' Quoted in *The Banner of Truth*, Aug/Sept. 2015, 27.

[2] From Macaulay's *Speeches* (1866), quoted by Francis Lyall in *Of Presbyters and Kings*, 25.

[3] Previously the Free Church only allowed psalms to be sung in services of worship without the accompaniment of musical instruments. (At one time there

plenary Assembly in November of that year, it was agreed (albeit by only 98 votes to 84) to give freedom for congregations to sing hymns and use musical accompaniment subject to the decision of the Kirk Session. This undoubtedly made it easier for some to join the Free Church.

However, there has not been a concerted course of action. It might be argued that there would have been more likelihood of such co-ordination if people had all stayed in the Church of Scotland until an agreed date, and some have argued that evangelicals who have left the denomination weakened the effort to resist the liberal trend. On the other hand, people have felt constrained and compelled to take action sooner rather than later. In terms of Bonhoeffer's illustration, they felt that it would be futile to simply run back through the compartments of a train that was speeding on in the wrong direction. The only thing to do was to get off the train.

One interesting and perhaps positive effect of the disparate responses is that there cannot be said to have been any kind of jumping on to a bandwagon. That might have been alleged if there had been a co-ordinated response. The very fact that so many individual ministers and members have taken the action they have taken underlines the significance and seriousness of their commitment as they have sought the right way forward for them and their congregations.

That seriousness can also be seen when we consider the social background. When the Disruption of 1843 took place after a long period of conflict, there was popular applause for the decision of so many to sacrifice so much for the sake of principle. This support can be seen, for example, in the events of the day. Although the General Assembly was not scheduled to commence until 2.30 pm on 18 May that year,

---

was a similar view in the Church of Scotland. When the congregation which I served was built in 1805, the Duke of Fife installed an organ, but it was only used during midweek family visits and was eventually donated to another church. It was almost a hundred years before another organ was built and used.)

> Between four and five in the morning, spectators filled the galleries at the St Andrew's Church in Edinburgh ... [and] as the morning progressed, thousands more gathered outside the Church; their presence confirmed the widespread expectation that this day would mark a decisive moment for the Scottish Church and society.[1]

This popular support was also related to other factors, such as the dislike of the land-owning classes by many of Scotland's small tenant farmers (as reflected in the classic north-east of Scotland tale of Johnny Gibb of Gushetneuk).[2]

By contrast, the stand many have taken in recent times is far from being popular. The homosexual lobby has been very successful in spreading the idea that practices which defy both common-sense and biology (let alone the teaching of the Bible) should be not only tolerated but celebrated. The opposing view is often widely regarded as intolerant and unloving, even if there remains a large segment of our society that regards homosexuality as unnatural but is afraid to say so. As recently as 2011, the Office of National Statistics reported (in *Civil Partnership Five Years On*) that the majority of people in Britain opposed same-sex 'marriage', but our Parliaments have pressed on regardless and have, they claim, 're-defined' marriage.

The point we are making is that the decision to leave the Church of Scotland over the issue of the admission of practising homosexual ministers does not have the same kind of popular support enjoyed by those who left the Church of Scotland at the time of the Disruption.

These factors highlight the serious nature and sometimes costly consequences of the decisions made by those who have left the

[1] S. J. Brown & M. Fry, eds., *Scotland in the Age of the Disruption* (Edinburgh University Press, 1993), vii.

[2] William Alexander, *Johnny Gibb of Gushetneuk* (Tuckwell Press edition, 1995). The cover blurb says that the novel 'tells of the struggle for democratic control which shattered the Church of Scotland in the great Disruption of 1843 and the parallel contest for control of the land between, on the one hand, the lairds and capitalistic muckle [large, powerful] farmers and, on the other, the cottars and smaller tenants'.

Kirk. Many ministers, elders and members have struggled hard to come to a decision about what to do, and there are some who strongly oppose the Assembly's repeated decisions but are still agonising over whether, when, and how to exit the denomination.

In some cases, ministers have individually resigned from the Church of Scotland and accepted a call to minister in another denomination (Free Church, Associated Presbyterian Church, United Free Church).

In other cases, new congregations have been formed as groups of members have left under their ministers who have resigned from the Church of Scotland. Some of these congregations have moved, pretty seamlessly, into the Free Church of Scotland, and others into the International Presbyterian Church. Some fellowships have not yet made a decision about which denomination to join and so remain temporarily independent, while among others there is talk of some kind of informal 'interdependence'. These developments are taking place within the context of a rejection of denominationalism, but they may lead to the formation of yet another denomination in Scotland. It has often been said that we have more than enough denominations in Scotland and, while it is obviously good for churches to be in gospel partnership, this should surely be regarded as an 'over and above' to their denominational affiliation – in the same way as churches may be part of, for example, the Evangelical Alliance as well as their own denomination.

One of the values of Presbyterian church government is that it combines equality (even a moderator has no more power than any other member) with an accountability structure. One of the questions put to ordinands in the Church of Scotland is: 'Do you acknowledge the Presbyterian government of this Church to be agreeable to the Word of God; and do you promise to be subject in the Lord to this Presbytery and to the superior courts of the Church and to take your due part in the administration of its affairs?' This is turn reflects the statement in *The Form of Church Government*, as approved by the Westminster Assembly:

> As there were in the Jewish church elders of the people joined with the priests and Levites in the government of the church, so Christ, who hath instituted government, and governors ecclesiastical in the church, hath furnished some in his church, beside the ministers of the word, with gifts for government, and with commission to execute the same when called thereunto, who are to join with the minister in the government of the church. Which officers reformed churches commonly call Elders.

The distinction many find in 1 Timothy 5:17, between 'the elders who rule well' and 'especially those who labour in preaching and teaching', lies behind the Presbyterian distinction between ruling elders and teaching elders. Where this distinction is not recognised and ministers regard themselves, and are regarded by others, as simply elders with the same authority as the others, the way is open for the 'control' and even dismissal of preachers by their fellow-elders, whereas a Presbyterian system regards ministers as chosen (and financially supported) by the congregation but admitted to their charge by the Presbytery, and it is to the Presbytery that they are responsible for the conduct of their ministry. This system offers a kind of protection for ministers and congregations from control by people or groups of people who may have a particular axe to grind.

Chapter 1 above spoke of both sadness and excitement. There has been much sadness, but there must surely be much excitement too, as we look in faith and hope to see what the living God will bring out of the turmoil of these times.

As I was gathering information for this book, an elder said to me that he and his fellow-elders have no regrets about their decision to leave the Church of Scotland. There may be regret that it has been necessary, but in all my contacts, I have not heard any expression of regret on the part of those who have left the denomination. That is not to say that there have been no problems; an easy exit could hardly have been expected. It has been difficult and sometimes costly, but one thing is clear – because we have it on the highest authority – Jesus Christ is building his church and the gates of hell will not prevail against it (Matt. 16:18). If we may borrow the words of an old hymn: 'Crowns and thrones may perish' and 'Kingdoms rise and wane' – and so do denominations – but the church of Jesus goes on; we have 'Christ's own promise and that cannot fail.'[1]

Foundations

An Australian home-owner came home one day to find that his house had collapsed; all that was left was a pile of dust and rubble. It transpired that, unbeknown to him, white ants has been eating away at the foundations and supporting timbers of the house for years. Everything had continued to look normal on the outside, but internally the house was being gradually consumed, until one day it crashed to the ground – destroyed by the tiny insects.[2]

This is an illustration of what has been happening both within Western civilisation and within the professing church for a long time. The Judaeo-Christian heritage and foundations of Western society have been subjected to such undermining under the influence of secularism, materialism, and multi-culturalism. At the same time many 'ants' have been at work within the church, calling in question teachings and practices that had been taken for granted for many generations.

The reference to foundations recalls the concluding words of the Sermon on the Mount, where Jesus contrasted wisdom and folly (Matt. 7:24-27). The wise man, he said, built his house on rock while the foolish man built his house on a sandy foundation. Obviously, in any building project the foundations are all-important. Jesus then spoke of floods and storms assailing the respective houses: while the one on the rock withstood every test, the one built on sand collapsed and great was its fall. What are these sandy foundations – or, more importantly what is the sure foundation

[1] Hymn, 'Onward, Christian Soldiers', by Sabine Baring-Gould (1834–1924).
[2] *Barnabas Aid*, May/June 2007, 2.

that will enable the house to stand? The crux of the matter is found in the stark contrast between 'Everyone who hears these words of mine and does them' and 'everyone who hears these words of mine and does not do them'.

Also to be found in the Sermon on the Mount, which is often lauded as a marvellous ethical treatise, Jesus said,

> Enter by the narrow gate. For the gate is wide and the way is easy that leads to destruction, and those who enter by it are many. For the gate is narrow and the way is hard that leads to life, and those who find it are few (Matt. 7:13-14).

He went on to speak about those who will enter the kingdom of heaven. For anyone who professes to follow Jesus it is vitally important to pay attention to his expressed teaching on such an issue. And what did he say? The one who will 'enter the kingdom of heaven' is 'the one who does the will of my Father who is in heaven'.

Does that conflict with all that is taught in Scripture about salvation by grace alone through faith alone? Not at all. Jesus himself told a parable about someone who simply prayed, 'God, be merciful to me, a sinner' (Luke 18:13) and who was 'justified'. That expression about those who do the Father's will bids us remember that while justification and salvation come by faith alone, such saving faith is never alone. There are certain things that 'accompany salvation' (Heb. 6:9; NIV) and in the verse before the one already quoted, Jesus said, 'You will recognise them by their fruits' (Matt. 7:20). As Martin Luther said, 'Good works do not make a man good, but a good man does good works.'[1]

Finally, let me set alongside each other the words of Psalm 127:1 and 1 Corinthians 15:58. The first text says, 'Unless the Lord builds the house, those who build it labour in vain.'[2] In the

[1] In *The Freedom of the Christian Man*, quoted in Bainton, *Here I Stand*, 178.

[2] Which is the historic motto of Scotland's capital city: '*Nisi Dominus frustra.*' (Recently the City of Glasgow has adopted the marketing slogan, 'People Make Glasgow' – a rather different message from the time-honoured, 'Let Glasgow Flourish', abbreviated as that was from the inscription on the Tron Church bell,

second text, Paul expresses the encouraging word, 'in the Lord your labour is not in vain'. The latter forms the final verse in a long chapter which sets forth the implications of the death and resurrection of Christ and the promise of future glory for his people – 'When the perishable puts on the imperishable and the mortal puts on immortality, then shall come to pass the saying that is written: "Death is swallowed up in victory."'

And, as with the Bible generally, things are not left 'up in the clouds' but on the solid ground of this earth in which God calls us to serve him in the meantime. The apostle writes, 'Therefore, my beloved brothers, be steadfast, immovable, always abounding in the work of the Lord, knowing that in the Lord your labour is not in vain.'

---

cast in 1631, 'Lord, let Glasgow flourish through the preaching of thy word and praising of thy name.')

8

A Selection of Stories and Testimonies

THIS final chapter incorporates a representative sample of stories we have been given. It is difficult to tell how many people have left the Church of Scotland over the issues discussed in this book; there may be many individuals or groups whose departure has been private and unheralded. Some congregations that are still in the denomination could tell of members who have simply 'walked' and who now worship and serve elsewhere. This is an ongoing story and I apologise to any individuals or groups whose stories we have not heard, and at the same time thank those who have contributed and helped in the preparation of this record.

Some of the following accounts have been edited: the full versions can be read online at banneroftruth.org (follow the link on the book information page of *A Sad Departure*), along with a moving personal testimony of a twenty-seven-year-old Christian about her battles with same-sex attraction.

Trinity Church, Aberdeen

In the May 2012 issue of *Evangelicals Now*, a front-page article reported that on 4 December 2011 'Trinity Church, Aberdeen was born. The new church fellowship was formed as a result of decisions taken by the Church of Scotland ...'

In 2011, the Rev. Peter Dickson had written to the members of High Hilton Church, where he had ministered for fifteen years: 'I have decided (after nearly three years of heart searching, discussion, negotiation and many meetings) that the best way in which to honour Christ and continue a gospel ministry is for me to demit my charge, leave High Church, Hilton, and, together with David Gibson, serve a new church family here in Aberdeen.' This was the first of the new congregations formed as a result of the recent decisions of the General Assembly.

He further wrote, 'In choosing to endorse ministers who are in same-sex relationships the Church of Scotland has, at the same time, chosen to make it impossible for me to continue in its ministry. That clear choice reveals two diametrically opposed views of the Bible and two incompatible understandings of the gospel. The Church of Scotland has acted in a schismatic way, separating itself from the worldwide church's historic understanding of the nature of the Bible, marriage and sexuality, and breaking fellowship with those who hold to Christ's teaching. Jesus said, "Whoever has my commandments and keeps them, he it is who loves me"' (John 14:21).

An elder and his wife provided a beautiful building at the bottom of their garden for a new office, and four members of staff were able to commence work in it straight away. David Gibson explained, 'When we announced our resignations we did not know where our new church would meet. In the end we found ourselves in the Northern Hotel, with very accommodating staff and all our requirements suitably met. We had to move our evening service to 5 pm due to the hotel's long-standing booking with other clients, but this has proved an attractive time for those with younger children to begin attending together.'

Within the Trinity church family there are people from varying backgrounds – Anglican, Baptist, Presbyterian, Pentecostal, Brethren – yet, as Galatians 3:28 says, all are one in Christ Jesus. At an early stage the decision was made to become a congregation of the International Presbyterian Church, and a building fund was established in September 2014 with a view to the eventual acquisition of permanent premises. At the time of writing, over £300,000 has been pledged over the next three years – which the elders regard as an encouraging start.

The Church, which has about 170 attending (membership 130), is led by the Kirk Session, two of whom were full-time ministers. One, Peter Dickson, resigned in late 2014 and the other, David Gibson – IPC's first ordinand in Scotland (ordained on 19 February 2012) – now serves as minister and pastor.

Highland International Church, Inverness

James Torrens has described the decision to leave the ministry of the Church of Scotland as the hardest decision of his life. Exchanging the world of medicine for the ministry of the word had been a tough call, but this decision was in a different league. Over time he became sure that God was calling him away, not just from the congregation of St Rollox in Sighthill, Glasgow, but from the Church of Scotland also. James announced his resignation on the 18 September 2011.

James wrote: 'Apart from the decisions being taken at a national level, events had a particular focus in Glasgow Presbytery. A member of Presbytery had admitted on the floor of Presbytery to having been in a civil partnership for some years and in a homosexual relationship for years before that. He made the observation that none of the roofs of the churches where he continued to lead worship had ever fallen in, implying that God was not particularly bothered about his lifestyle.

'A few of us sought to use the proper procedural mechanisms in Presbytery to respond to this public display of defiance of the word of God and the laws of the Church. But over the next year it became clear that there was no appetite either in the committees and courts of the Church or among evangelicals in Glasgow Presbytery to discipline, in love, the individual concerned.'

In June 2011, James informed the elders and congregation that it was unlikely that he would be able to continue for much longer as a minister in the Church of Scotland. 'When I announced my demission in September 2011, I did not know where I was going to go or what I was going to do. It was time to put into practice the *obedience of faith* as outlined in Hebrews 11:8 (NIV), a verse which hung on my study wall: "By faith Abraham, when called ... obeyed and went, even though he did not know where he was going."

In October that year James was invited to meet up in Glasgow with representatives of the International Presbyterian Church and he was asked if he would consider going to Inverness to minister God's word to a new group, consisting of a number of Christians who were unhappy with the position and direction of the Church of Scotland. Most, though not all, were members of Kinmylies Church of Scotland where Peter Humphris had been minister for over ten years. (Peter had demitted his status as a Church of Scotland minister on 7 February 2012, four months before he was due to retire.) The congregation of Highland International Church held its first gathering for public worship at the Best Western Palace Hotel on 1 April 2012.

Grace Community Church, Kyle of Lochalsh

John Murdo Macdonald had had misgivings about the direction which the Church of Scotland had been taking with regard to the authority of God's word for a number of years, and matters came to a head for him in 2009. He was appointed by Lochcarron & Skye Presbytery to be part of a group of three who were to present an Overture to the 2009 General Assembly in opposition to the proposed induction of a practising homosexual as minister of a congregation in Aberdeen.

That Overture was overtaken by a motion to appoint a Special Commission to look into the issue of same-sex partnerships in the ministry. 'With reluctance we agreed to withdraw, and the General Assembly agreed both the said induction and the setting up of the Special Commission.'

Prior to leaving for the 2011 General Assembly, at which he was a Commissioner, he informed the Kirk Session that if the vote went against the evangelical position there was a distinct possibility that he would leave the Church of Scotland, and on his return he informed the Session that he and the Church of Scotland would be parting company.

'I spent the next six months explaining my position to the congregation. I explained that I could no longer with any integrity receive a stipend from the Church and live in the manse while at the same time feeling so strongly about what had happened, and indeed preaching from God's word against the path which the Church had chosen to take. I made clear that the call on my life to preach the gospel came from Christ, and that when the Church denied him and his word, my allegiance had to be with Christ. I also made clear that each and every member and adherent had a responsibility before God to make their own decision, and I urged people to show love and understanding towards those of different opinions.'

In October 2011, Mr Macdonald informed his Presbytery Clerk of his decision to demit his charge on 31 December that year – 'one of the most difficult and heart-rending decisions I have ever had to take. I remember sitting in front of the computer for about ten minutes before I finally, prayerfully pressed the "Send" key.

'About half the congregation (approximately thirty-five people) decided to leave the Church of Scotland with me, and a new church fellowship was established in South Skye and Lochalsh, with a view to providing a place of worship for those people who felt that they could no longer support the Church of Scotland.

'The new fellowship met for the first time on 1 January 2012 in Kyle Primary School with about fifty people attending. In March three of us travelled to London to represent the congregation at the Presbytery meeting of the International Presbyterian Church in Ealing and on Sunday 11 March the congregation voted unanimously to call me as their minister. Later that month it was agreed that the congregation would be named Grace Community Church, a congregation of the International Presbyterian Church.

'At the time of writing, we look back and thank God for his ongoing presence, provision and blessing; we have seen established a congregation of forty-two members and fifteen adherents together with over twenty young folk coming along regularly to worship. We have run Christianity Explored, Discipleship Explored, and Alpha Courses, and have seen many come to engage with the gospel through these courses. We continue to run a Road to Recovery Group which helps people struggling with addictions and dependencies. We have also established a local Christians Against Poverty Debt Centre which has been a great witness in the community, and we have been involved, together with other local churches, in the setting up of a Foodbank. Through these outreaches about twenty families have been touched by the grace and love of God in Jesus. And above all we have seen fourteen people come to a saving knowledge of the Lord. That to us is the ultimate proof of God's presence – only he can save souls and set us free from sin. To God be the glory.'

The Tron Church, Glasgow

In May 2011 Rev. William Philip wrote about the decisions of that year's General Assembly: 'Where does this leave our church fellowship in St George's-Tron? Alas, it seems, greatly at odds with the clearly expressed official will of the denomination to which we are affiliated. But, notwithstanding the deliberations and decisions of the highest court of our denomination, we are simply not at liberty to walk away from Christ and his gospel or depart from the historic foundations of our Church or separate from communion with orthodox Christian believers globally. To do so would be sin against God, and sin against our Christian brothers and sisters worldwide, many of whom are facing great persecution for their adherence to the truth. This we cannot do. We must obey God rather than men.'

Former Session Clerk, Tom Magill, supplied the following summary of the Tron's story.

'Biblical ministry has characterised the Tron for many years, and the beliefs of the congregation have reflected this: a metropolitan, gathered congregation, comprising folk from many denominations, new converts, many from overseas, and not a few rescued from a life of addiction. Whatever their personal history, faithfulness to the Bible is the *sine qua non* of belief and congregational loyalty.

'Buchanan Street is the second busiest shopping street in the United Kingdom, and the Tron was "a church in the heart of the city with the city in its heart". It needed to be a welcoming place seven days per week to those who would never darken the door of a church. There they could meet to hear the gospel in a variety of non-traditional encounters. This spiritual imperative was the indispensable, and only, driver for a major refurbishment programme initiated in 2007. Some £3,000,000 for the new facilities was pledged, with a tithe of the construction cost to be set aside for gospel work elsewhere. Unforeseen structural problems costing £600,000 led to the need for bridging finance, and a loan of £750,000 was secured from the General Trustees of the Church of Scotland at commercial rates. Repayment by instalments was scheduled to the end of 2015. The work was completed in 2009.'

Mr Magill then refers to the decisions of the 2011 General Assembly, described by the Minister as 'a resounding defeat for those like ourselves who were committed to the orthodox, historic, Christian gospel'. The Kirk Session followed with a statement declaring that it found itself in 'impaired fellowship', unable to contribute funds or to recognize oversight of, or participate in meetings of, the Kirk structures. Meetings were held with the Presbytery Clerk and the General Trustees to seek a reasonable agreement whereby the building could be retained. These meetings initially were amicable and a clear expectation was given that, with suitable financial arrangements, a settlement would be reached by March 2012, including the settlement of debts. A general meeting of the congregation was held in November 2011 which was attended by 247 members; a vote of confidence in the Session's plans was carried by 96%.

'However, in early 2012 Presbytery requested a meeting with the Tron membership, issuing a letter to the members on the Roll, inviting attendance at a meeting on 7 March in order for the Church of Scotland to hear the views of the congregation. Two hundred and seventy-four members attended the meeting with representatives of Glasgow Presbytery along with officials from 121 George Street, Edinburgh[1] (Principal Clerk, Solicitor and Chair of General Trustees). It was a very unpleasant affair, with allegations made by those visiting of bullying, intimidation and misinformation against our leadership.

'After the Presbytery decided that negotiations should not be continued and that another Special Committee be set up to investigate the possibility of creating a new congregation in our building, the Session resolved unanimously that the congregation would formally secede from the Church of Scotland. The congregation then approved a new constitution by 217 votes to 2, and next day Presbytery was informed. We also informed The Charity Regulator of our removal from the denomination. A few days later we discovered that '121' had managed to have frozen all our bank accounts without telling us.

'The Cohesiveness Group reported to Presbytery in June that it was "deeply disappointing that the congregation had unilaterally seceded, without first settling the debts of some £1,000,000". This was misinformation, £500,000 being the outstanding loan to the General Trustees, a liability on a building they themselves were claiming as their asset, and in any case a future liability since it was not due for repayment until 2015. Every payment had been made to the date of our secession, and indeed on the day following our vote to secede the Minister and Session Clerk personally handed over the one outstanding loan payment to the Chairman of the General Trustees as a gesture of good faith that we might still, despite all, be able to reach a negotiated and reasonable settlement. The remainder of the alleged £1,000,000 was a supposed accumulated "shortfall" in Mission & Aid Fund allocations going

[1] The address of the Church of Scotland's main office.

back years, which we had vigorously disputed and many previous meetings with Presbytery had already conceded was totally unrealistic.'

The Presbytery also decided to take action to protect the interests of the remaining members, to appoint office bearers, and to consult with the Council of Assembly to investigate the probity and integrity of the Trustees of St George's Tron. This report was approved, and an announcement was placed in *The Herald* newspaper, inviting members who wished to remain in the denomination to a meeting on 24 June 2012. Five people turned up, only one of whom was on the Roll of St George's Tron, but the Presbytery resolved to appoint a Transition Minister to rebuild the congregation, make effective use of the building and recover all assets – even though not a single member of the congregation remained in the building in Buchanan Street.

The last service at the Tron was held on the morning of 9 December 2012, and the new congregation met that evening in 25 Bath Street with 'an overwhelming sense of liberation and joy'.

Reflecting on all that has happened, Mr Magill reports that two remarkable factors have emerged from this crisis. One is that the congregation has remained united throughout; not one member has chosen to stay with 'the artificial Church of Scotland gathering in the Buchanan Street building. Never has the fellowship been stronger, more vigorous and more focussed on the gospel than it is today.' The second reflection is that the Lord has provided accommodation. 'The Bath Street Halls had been declared in May 2009 to be surplus to the Glasgow Presbytery Plan, and the Session had been instructed that the building must be disposed of within ten years. Providentially, Cornhill Scotland bought the premises, and so the Tron and Cornhill Scotland were provided with a home to continue their ministry in the city centre. Today the congregation is in the midst of rebuilding work to fit the building for ongoing and expanding ministry in the city centre of Glasgow, and planning further growth into other parts of the city.'

Grace Church, Larbert

Andrew Randall was ordained and inducted at Larbert Old Church in June 2009, following the faithful twenty-three-year ministry of the Rev. Cliff Rennie and a few weeks after the 2009 General Assembly. The congregation had had a history of biblical ministry stretching back to the 1970s and as a result the vast majority of the Kirk Session and congregation were in no doubt about the wrongness of the decisions of the General Assemblies of 2009, 2011, and 2013. The real question throughout those years was how to respond in a manner which was faithful and Christ-exalting. This is Mr Randall's account of their journey.

'As with many other congregations of Reformed convictions, we had to feel our way through a myriad of issues. The potential significance of the Kirk's rejection of Scripture was immediately apparent and over the following four years, a number of congregational meetings were held, various statements were issued, and the congregation was kept advised of developments through regular articles in the church magazine.

'Throughout that period we sought to play our part in making clear to the denomination the potential ramifications of its continuing down the path it had chosen. Following the General Assembly decisions of 2011, we withdrew from cooperation with the courts and committees of the Church of Scotland and suspended payments to central funds beyond the costs of our own ministry. We also brought these issues before the Lord constantly in prayer, including establishing a separate weekly prayer meeting (in addition to our existing one) specifically relating to this issue.

'Historically, Larbert Old Church had a difficult relationship with the Presbytery of Falkirk stemming particularly from the fact that the Kirk Session consisted of men only. The Presbytery had previously alienated the congregation through a particularly inappropriate and aggressive quinquennial visit.

'From the summer of 2011 onwards our relationship with the Presbytery deteriorated further, particularly as its officers sought to use various procedural mechanisms to disrupt the life of the congregation and undermine the elders' authority. Resisting these efforts was immensely draining in terms of time and spiritual energy, and increasingly so as time passed. The spiritual nature of the battle could not have been clearer.

'Many elders were inclined to leave the Church of Scotland after May 2011, but it was decided to await the 2013 decision, although only on the basis that we would use the intervening period to consider what our destination might be if we did choose to leave the Kirk. We considered that question carefully over a period of around eighteen months, before deciding that we would seek affiliation with the International Presbyterian Church.

'In May 2012 the General Assembly rejected a proposed resolution seeking to clarify that church premises should only be used for Christian (rather than non-Christian) worship. This further intensified our sense of alienation from our own denomination and our uneasiness of conscience at remaining a part of it.

'Throughout this time, the work of the congregation continued as the elders sought and articulated a vision for the future of gospel ministry in the area. One of the wonderful things about our experience was to see great blessing from God, with a significantly growing congregation and a growing hunger for the word, at the same time as things were becoming more and more difficult in our relationship with our denomination. In particular, our Sunday School multiplied several times over as new families came to faith and others joined the church. These were much-needed encouragements in difficult days.

'After the 2013 General Assembly's decision to approve the ordination of practising homosexuals, the final decision to leave the denomination was simultaneously very easy and immensely difficult. It was an enormous relief finally to reach this point and intimate it to the congregation. By this time, following some resignations, we had around twenty elders on the Kirk Session. Fifteen indicated their intention to leave. At the time of this announcement in June 2013 we had no concrete arrangements in place for a new church. What we were clear about was that this initiative would be led by the elders, who we believed had this God-given responsibility.

'On Sunday 25 August, Grace Church Larbert held its first services in a local school. An attendance of around 200 that day, including some extra supporters, gave way to a normal weekly attendance of 140-160 at the morning service and 60-80 in the evening. Approximately three quarters of the worshipping congregation from Larbert Old joined Grace Church Larbert. The prayer meeting and youth work were able to continue without interruption through the generosity of a local mission hall, the Dawson Mission, the office-bearers of which graciously allowed the new congregation to use their premises in a spirit of gospel unity.

'In conclusion, this has been a period of rich blessing, sweet unity and great anticipation. The congregation has grown in that time and we now have around 140 adults and 60 young people associated with the Church. Our youth ministry has been reinvigorated, our work with teenagers is flourishing as never before, and the congregation continues to give major support to a local interdenominational youth project. A new small group ministry was launched in 2014 and has been much appreciated, as has the new 5th Larbert Company of the Boys' Brigade, formed by officers who belong to the congregation and the local Baptist Church. The congregation has been generous in its giving, allowing for the purchase of a manse on a 50-50 joint equity arrangement with minister and congregation. We have now introduced a part-time assistant, and are well under way in raising funds to buy or build a new permanent home for the church family.'

Grace Church, Dundee

Grace Church began its life on 22 September 2013 after departing from the congregation of Logie & St John's (Cross).

In June 2012, the Kirk Session of Logie & St John's (Cross) Church issued a statement to members of the congregation about the decisions of the General Assemblies of 2009 and 2011 which placed the Church of Scotland on 'a trajectory in regard to the issue of same-sex relationships and the ministry which rejects the authority of God's word and resists the Kingship and Headship of the Lord Jesus Christ whose good and gracious rule among his people is exercised through obedience to that word. It is these decisions which have plunged the denomination into a crisis.'

Before the 2013 Assembly, the Session issued another letter to members, including the reaffirmation that '... deep pain and sadness notwithstanding, leaving the Church of Scotland is still a real possibility if the revisionist trajectory is pursued but we want to do so in the unity of the Spirit, as a church family, mindful that the enemy would love nothing better than to sow discord.'

The Rev. David Scott left Logie & St John's at the end of April that year and, after the self-contradictory decision of the 2013 General Assembly, the members of the Kirk Session stood together on the church chancel and the following statement was read out: 'After further deliberation at its meeting on 5 June 2013 and taking into account last Sunday's congregational meeting, the Kirk Session has firmly decided to find an appropriate means for this congregation to leave the Church of Scotland.'

On Sunday 18 August a further document was distributed, which said: 'The Kirk Session unanimously agree that this decision is a clear affront to our risen Saviour and Lord Jesus Christ who said, "Whoever has my commands and keeps them is the one who loves me", and unless the Church of Scotland experiences reformation and a return to its 400-year heritage of submitting to God's word, the Bible, we see no future for ourselves within the denomination.'

The same document, however, revealed the fact that some elders had changed their minds and felt that 'this fight can be conducted from within the denomination in the courts of the General Assembly and (we) will continue a congregation within Logie & St John's (Cross) Church'. The statement intimated that on 22 September the new Grace Church would meet for the first time but that others would remain in the Church of Scotland.

Arrangements were made to meet in the Menzieshill Community Centre, and Grace Church began its life on 22 September 2013, with an attendance of about 90 in the morning and 40 in the evening. The author of this book had submitted his resignation from the ministry of the Church of Scotland to Dundee Presbytery and, after a lifetime's involvement in the Church of Scotland, stepped into new territory as *Locum* of the newly-birthed church. A sense of excitement permeated the fellowship of the congregation. The provision of facilities for Sunday services and for the Wednesday Prayer Meetings (which alternated with house-groups) was providential and a strong sense of family togetherness was evident. People willingly co-operated in various practical expressions of Christian concern: the Thursday 'Bowl 'n' Roll' soup lunches, Christians Against Poverty and the Raven Trust (aid to Malawi). After an initial year of consolidation, the church believed it was time to call a pastor and in August 2014 Mark Ellis took up this position.

Christ Church, Edinburgh

The Rev. David Court has been in the ministry for more than 25 years, first in Glasgow and, since the year 2000, in Edinburgh. He has written:

> Many years ago Francis Schaeffer wrote: 'Once Christ is no longer King and Lord in a church, then that church cannot have our loyalty. When a church comes to the place where it can no longer exert discipline, then with tears before the Lord we must consider a second step. If the battle for doctrinal purity is lost … it may be necessary for true Christians to leave the visible organisation with which they have been associated. But note well: if we must leave our church, it should always be with tears – not with drums playing and flags flying.'

Mr Court demitted the pastoral charge of New Restalrig and left the Church of Scotland on 30 September 2013. About 80 members associated themselves with St Columba's Free Church of Scotland and started a new congregation, Christ Church, Edinburgh. 'I can assure you there were no drums playing, nor any flags flying!'

Posing the question of what led the members of New Restalrig to secede from the Church of Scotland, a denomination of which Mr Court himself had been part for almost his whole life, he answered: 'I have been a Church of Scotland minister for almost exactly twenty years and in that time I have attended General Assemblies both as a commissioner and as a corresponding member. I must say that I have never before been so ashamed to be a Church of Scotland minister as at this Assembly.'

The decisions of the General Assemblies of 2009, 2011 and 2013 in relation to ministers and same-sex relationships ultimately led New Restalrig's Kirk Session to seek an exit from the Church of Scotland. A congregational meeting was held in May 2013 at which it was clear that the overwhelming majority of the Kirk Session and active congregation wished to leave the Church of Scotland.

'At a meeting in June all members of the Kirk Session present expressed their intention to leave the Church of Scotland and, God-willing, form a new congregation in order to honour Christ and continue a clear gospel witness within the local community, and on 6 October 2013 that new church came into being. We now meet in a different building and we are part of a different denomination. It has not been easy; leaving a building is neither here nor there, but leaving behind some of our brothers and sisters was hard. However, for the most part we left on good terms and with no bitter feelings or harsh words. We simply had to do what God had asked of us.

'A sad departure? Yes but the sadness was not really in having to leave the denomination with which many of us had been associated for decades. The sadness rather continues to be in the departure of that denomination from the one holy, catholic and apostolic faith.'

Hope Church, Kirkmuirhill, South Lanarkshire

Kirkmuirhill Church of Scotland was a congregation with a long evangelical history, an all-male eldership, and a membership that was becoming increasingly distressed about the denomination's theological trajectory.

The Rev. Ian Watson was for a time Secretary of *Forward Together* and was often asked to comment on church affairs, appearing on television and radio and representing the evangelical position in the newspapers. Throughout that period the members of the congregation were very supportive of their minister. Prayer meetings were held during the Assembly debates. The Kirkmuirhill congregation was in a unique situation in terms of the title to their church property.

'Originally a United Presbyterian congregation, the feu disposition was also a trust deed vesting title in local trustees on behalf of the congregation. Two clauses envisaged divisions in the congregation. Although our initial legal advice turned out to be misleading, in the end we clarified that if three-quarters of the congregation voted to adhere together the property would be held on their behalf irrespective of denominational allegiance.

'All eighteen elders were opposed to the idea of anyone in an active same-sex relationship being in the ministry, although two of them were adamant that they would not leave the Church of Scotland. The Session called a congregational meeting in advance of the General Assembly and informed the congregation that, should the Assembly confirm the revisionist trajectory, they intended to resign as elders and would ballot the congregation as to their future denominational home, assuring the congregation that if we stuck together we would be able to retain the building. There was a feeling among the Session that the congregation was generally supportive.

'The Session met again after the compromise decision of the 2013 Assembly and they were clear that that decision had not changed anything. They informed the congregation that a vote would be held in late June to determine the mind of the membership. Then a few members contacted Presbytery, who ordered the ballot stopped on pain of discipline. A meeting with Presbytery representatives, the Principal Clerk and the Church Solicitor resulted in an agreement to postpone the ballot on the understanding that there would be an attempt to reach a mutually agreeable solution. However, from then on the situation deteriorated. Presbytery held meetings for those who opposed the Session and as the year went on the numbers attending the meetings increased as the Presbytery encouraged those who wished to remain in the Church of Scotland and coached them for the congregational meetings called by Presbytery.'

Eventually, in December 2013 the Presbytery organised what it called an indicative ballot to determine the mind of the congregation. While the result showed a majority in favour of leaving the Church of Scotland, the percentage fell short of the three-quarters required in order to retain the buildings.

'The Session therefore began the search for an alternative place to worship for those who wished to leave the Church of Scotland, and from then on the story becomes one of blessing after blessing: a gift of £50,000 was received; an offer of free accommodation for the minister and his family for as long as they needed it; sacrificial giving on specially appointed Gift Days; the provision of the Community Centre for Sunday morning services and the Bowling Club for evening worship; the purchase of a manse directly opposite the Community Centre; identification of land as the possible site of a future building.

'The Session decided to hold a ballot in January 2014 which would satisfy the terms of the title deed. The result was that the congregation was split down the middle—140 for leaving, 140 for remaining. I indicated my intention to demit and resign my status as a Church of Scotland minister. During the process I had been in touch with the Free Church of Scotland and was accepted by them as a minister in March 2014. The Free Church has been very supportive and very kind both to me personally and to the congregation and we obtained official status as a settled congregation in March 2015.

'The process of leaving the Church of Scotland has been harrowing, but those of us who have left feel a tremendous sense of freedom. If we have suffered it has been for Christ's sake and that is a privilege. Worshipping in a gym hall and a club house, we have been forced to think differently about church. One of the surprising results has been the support from those outside our congregation. We have received a number of substantial financial gifts from others who admire the stand we have taken for Christ and this has been most encouraging.'

Broughty Ferry Presbyterian Church

The Rev. Alberto de Paula, who had been minister of St James' Parish Church in Broughty Ferry since 2005, informed the Presbytery of Dundee that he planned to demit his charge on 10 August 2014. He recalls the sadness of the last service in St James'. The family moved house on 14 August and on Sunday 17 August the new church – Broughty Ferry Presbyterian Church – began services of worship.

'St James', Broughty Ferry had been under evangelical ministry since the arrival of the Rev. Malcolm Ritchie in the mid-1950s. Many came to faith during his ministry. After his departure the Rev. Tom Robertson worked for about thirty years, consolidating St James' as an evangelical congregation.'

Mr de Paula continued that work. When the decision of the 2013 Assembly came, none of the elders had any doubt about opposing it, and the minister informed the Kirk Session of his decision to leave the Church of Scotland in about a year's time, asking the elders to make up their own minds on the matter. This gave a substantial period of notice for all interested parties to make arrangements in preparation for the minister's departure. There and then, one of the elders, speaking on behalf of Session, asked Mr de Paula whether he would be willing to become the minister of a new congregation made up of former members of St James' who would secede from the Church of Scotland.

After some weeks pondering it, he decided to say 'Yes' without stipulating any conditions such as housing, salary, or any other things which ministers generally expect to be in place for them. In view of that, St James' Session unanimously recommended that the whole congregation leave the Church of Scotland.

However, Mr de Paula writes: 'What had seemed to be a consensual matter soon proved to be a controversial one. There was the issue of a lifelong relationship with the buildings. The prospect of no longer worshipping in those premises would be too much for some. Others, despite over fifty years of evangelical ministry, would still pay allegiance to the Church of Scotland regardless of what decisions it took. And there were those who preferred to continue to carry on a faithful ministry within the Kirk without any radical change. For many, I think, the fear of being branded as "homophobes" was too much to bear.

'During that transitional year church activities ran as normally as possible. There was a meeting with representatives of Presbytery in January 2014, after which the Session appointed an action group to explore and prepare a departure for the sake of those who were definitely leaving. The group met every other week going through a list of more than 35 items, making provision for the formation of a new church. Presbytery assured those willing to stay that there would be support for the church to carry on and that, for the next five years they would not put the church under review, but the departure of the minister would mean that the church would no longer be allowed to call another until some form of adjustment were agreed (i.e. linkage or union).

'On that same day, Presbytery was informed that I would demit my charge after Sunday 10 August. This gave time to plan and prepare for running the church after that date. The last morning service had an atmosphere of sadness; the sermon was on the passage in Acts where Paul and Barnabas had to part company because of strong disagreement. The congregation was dismissed with the usual blessing. Monday came with the feeling that a heavy burden had been lifted from our shoulders.'

On 17 August the new church was born, with over 100 people present and many messages of support from all over Scotland. There are about 65 communicant members, plus children and teenagers, with an average attendance of some 80 or 90 people at morning services. The new congregation longs to grow as its members share the gospel in their community. Thanks to the generosity of some members, a manse was made available and a new home has been found for the new church in the town's main street.

Holyrood Evangelical Church, Edinburgh

The decision of the elders of Holyrood Abbey Church to leave the Church of Scotland was taken slowly, prayerfully and reluctantly. Some elders felt that the congregation should remain in the Kirk and stand for biblical truth; others felt that, while there was a case for leaving the Church of Scotland, they should wait until the final decision of the General Assembly had been made before doing so. Yet others were persuaded of the need to secede and willing to do so at the earliest opportunity.

The Rev. Philip Hair asked Euan Dodds, an elder (and Outreach Co-ordinator) of Holyrood Evangelical Church, to provide an account of subsequent developments.

'After the 2011 Assembly the elders intimated to the congregation and to Presbytery that they were unhappy at the course the Church of Scotland was taking. However, it was felt best to wait until the Theological Commission report and debate in 2013. Shortly after that Assembly, a Session meeting was called to consider the outcome, which was seen by many in Holyrood as a desperately unhappy, last-minute, attempt at compromise with a primary focus on preserving unity.

'After much prayer the elders unanimously agreed that they should begin the difficult process of leaving the denomination. Some had been in the Kirk – indeed in Holyrood Abbey – all their Christian lives. They had been baptized there, come to faith there, married there, been sent out from there to minister at home and abroad, had the funerals of loved ones there, seen their children baptized and married there. Others had family members who were committed to staying in. In time one elder would leave for another denomination (for various personal reasons) and one eventually chose to remain within the Kirk.

'It was only seven years since the members of the congregation had themselves raised upwards of £1.6 million to build a state-of-the-art church hall which accommodated a full range of midweek ministries. Most members, however, were quite prepared to count the cost of leaving.

'The same views expressed by elders could be found within the congregation: "stay in and fight", "wait a little longer", "leave now". The elders explained their decision and invited the congregation to follow their lead.

'The interactions with the Presbytery of Edinburgh were invariably awkward but usually cordial. The representatives of the Presbytery Cohesiveness Group were not impressed with our stance and reminded us of our obligations as charity trustees and elders who had vowed to seek the peace and unity of the Church. However, they did not stand in our way and sometimes offered helpful guidance on what needed to be done before our departure.'

To begin with a small group of elders was told that there might be the option of renting the building once Presbytery had a clear idea of how many were leaving. Later, however, and before there was any indication of whether some might stay, it was announced that the buildings would be retained for the Church of Scotland's use.

'It became clear to the congregation that the *status quo* was no longer an option. People could either follow the lead of their minister and elders – confident of the kind of ministry that would continue, albeit in an unknown location – or they could throw in their lot with Presbytery, remain in the church building for a period but face the uncertainty of what sort of ministry they would receive, or whether they would be united with another congregation, and one perhaps with a different theological emphasis. In the end, a small number remained in the Church of Scotland while the vast majority of the congregation left to found Holyrood Evangelical Church. The new church meets in Leith Academy on Sunday mornings and Portobello Town Hall on Sunday evenings.

'We have benefited immensely from the support of another seceding congregation, Chalmers Church, who have provided us with office space, the use of their photocopier, and premises for a prayer meeting. We still have the two questions of accommodation (where we might meet more permanently) – and affiliation (which denomination or grouping might we join). Great wisdom is needed in the days ahead.'

Writing four months after their departure, Mr Dodds has said that the decision to leave the denomination and the building was not easy but the seceders were delivered from sentimentality. The Sunday services are identical in all but venue, and the same commitment to midweek house-groups and prayer meetings goes on. A small number of new people have come along to services. Door-to-door work has started in Portobello and the congregation is getting acquainted with other churches in the area.

'There is grief over the state of the Church of Scotland – and sadness that some, while forever brothers and sisters in Christ, could not follow the lead of the elders into safer pastures. Some of the older saints have found the move unsettling and there have been discomforts and difficulties along the way. The emotional wounds are beginning to heal but the scar may take years to fade. Nonetheless, we do not look back in anger but fix our eyes on Jesus, the author and perfecter of our faith who for the joy set before him endured the cross (Heb. 12:2).'

North Harris Free Church, Outer Hebrides

In February 2014 the elders of Tarbert Church responded to the decision of the 2013 General Assembly in a document that was circulated among members of the congregation. They argued that the 'compromise decision' of the Assembly was incoherent in that it sought to uphold the traditional biblical view of sexual relationships and at the same time allow congregations to call ministers in same-sex partnerships. This decision, it was stated, 'is untruthful by its very nature, trying to hold together two completely opposing views as if they were compatible'. The elders also wrote, 'We do not believe the orientation to be attracted to the same sex is of itself sinful. What the Bible teaches is, however, very clear: same-sex sexual practice is sinful. ... If this decision is confirmed, the Church of Scotland, for the first time, formally in its laws and regulations, will have rejected the Bible and the gospel on an issue where the Bible is completely clear and consistent.'

Various meetings were held and, after much prayer and with great sadness, the elders announced plans to dissociate from the Church of Scotland and seek affiliation with another Presbyterian denomination. They also expressed the hope that those people who had expressed the desire to remain in the Church of Scotland would nonetheless come with the majority so that the church family would stay together.

In August 2014 the Moderator of the Church of Scotland Presbytery of Uist issued a 'personal appeal to members and adherents of Tarbert' to remain within the Church of Scotland. While expressing strong disagreement with the 'shameful decision' of the Assembly, he wrote, 'I do not find any authority in the New Testament to justify a response of leaving the Church of Scotland and dividing a faithful and God-honouring congregation.'

In response to the appeal, and in particular to the view that secession would be harmful to unity, the elders argued that, on the contrary, 'the idea of moving to another denomination ... is an act of solidarity with our fellow evangelicals in the western isles'.

They pointed out that the decision to secede was not a knee-jerk reaction but one which had taken years of heart-searching and prayer. 'It is not about being anti-gay. It is about the way our denomination has abandoned truth. The statements by the Church of Scotland supporting the traditional views on sexuality are false – they have abandoned the traditional biblical view.'

Writing about the possibility of becoming a congregation of the Free Church, it was pointed out that the Free Church holds to 'the truth of Scripture and provides a home for an evangelical congregation that can only be beneficial'; they even argued, 'If we all join the Free Church there will be one less denomination in North Harris and therefore greater outward unity.'

In October 2014 about 100 members and adherents left the Church of Scotland to form North Harris Free Church, with the Rev. Roddy Morrison serving initially as Locum. He had demitted his status as a minister of the Church of Scotland in February 2012 and joined the Free Church in October of that year. He speaks of the buoyancy and the spirit of joyful worship in the new congregation meeting in the village hall. The title deeds of the church building were in the name of the Deacons' Court and, since the members of the Church of Scotland did not all leave, the Church of Scotland claimed the buildings. However, according to Mr Morrison, once the seceders 'gave up their buildings and walked out, they told me that it was as if a burden had been lifted from them. They were convinced that they took the right action' in not pursuing issues legally. The new church has ten elders and two deacons. On 10 February 2015 the Rev. David Macleod, who had resigned from the Church of Scotland (Applecross, Lochcarron & Torridon), was inducted as minister of North Harris Free Church.

West Church, Inverness

Andrew McMillan was converted in the year 2000 while serving in the Royal Marines. He then attended his local parish church in Denny where he benefited from 'the faithful expository ministry of an evangelical man who had a deep love for Christ and desire for people to know God in his fulness'. He became a member and then an elder, before sensing a call to ministry. After completing his studies at the University of Edinburgh, he was ordained and inducted to Dalneigh and Bona (Inverness) at the beginning of 2012. He resigned in February 2015 and is now minister of the newly-formed Inverness West Free Church. He has written:

'In the Church of Scotland I have encountered and been influenced by many men who have spoken about the need to contend for the faith in the midst of a "broad church". Perhaps naively, I believed that there was still a glimmer of hope for the reformation of the denomination, and I gratefully accepted a call from Dalneigh and Bona, a charge with a noted history of evangelical ministry.

'From the beginning of my ministry there I was greatly heartened by the mindset of the many godly people and their zeal for God and his glory. Like me they were grateful for all that God had done in the denomination and embraced the rich Christian heritage of the Kirk. As we discussed the same-sex relationship issue, it became more and more clear that *our* understanding of the nature of the Scriptures – which is in line with Christian faith throughout the last 2,000 years – was simply not shared by the majority of our denomination, which has chosen to listen instead to the spirit of the age rather than the Spirit of Christ. The situation deeply grieved us all, and for me my future in the Church of Scotland was uncertain.

'It was evident from the General Assembly's decision in 2013 to adopt the so-called "mixed economy" that this would distance us from the doctrine taught in Scripture.' Mr McMillan believed that, with the erosion of Reformed orthodoxy and a disregard for the authority, sufficiency and clear teaching of Scripture he could no longer remain as a minister of the Kirk in good conscience. 'When the reformation marks of a true church are neither present nor practised it becomes virtually impossible to be a true minister with real integrity. In setting this fatal course, the Kirk was indicating that there are no longer any institutional restraints to prevent a succession of deviations – moral, theological, and ecclesiastical – in the years ahead. There has been a failure to recognise that the Lord reigns through his word (Psa. 110:2; Isa. 11:4); no one has authority above Christ and no one has authority alongside him. He alone has the right to determine what will be done in his church.

'The Church of Scotland, by virtue of its General Assembly decisions, has gone beyond the word of the Lord. Neither is it listening to God himself revealed in Scripture, but instead creating a god based on the projections of flawed human minds. And one thing has always remained firmly in my mind: "We must obey God rather than men" (Acts 5:29). I personally must obey God rather than submit myself to a denomination that has left biblical truth for heretical but politically correct teachings. I therefore made the painful decision to leave. I have always been of the firm conviction that leaders have a responsibility to lead.

'Over the course of 2014 much discussion took place about whether it was viable for me to lead the congregation out of the Church of Scotland with a view to joining the Free Church of Scotland. Sadly, it became clear that there was unrest in the congregation, but I and many others believed that God was calling us to do something new in faithfulness to him, for the glory of his name and for the sake of Inverness and beyond.

'While I planned to demit formally in February 2015, a number of elders had resolved to establish an entirely new church in the west of Inverness as of 1 March 2015 (associated with the Free Church of Scotland), and had asked me to serve as minister of the new congregation. I accepted and, at the time of writing, West Church Inverness has been blessed with a congregation of approximately 80 people who made the painful decision to take a stand and leave the Church of Scotland. We were very grieved at the painful decision we all had to take, but we are also so grateful for God's provision and blessing as we look forward with a real sense of anticipation to what God may be preparing to do in these days.

'I thank Almighty God for the privilege of being able to serve Christ and his gospel in Dalneigh and Bona, and I continue pray that each one remaining will know the eternal riches of his grace through repentance and faith in his Son Jesus Christ. Finally, I am grateful for the opportunity of being able to leave with others, albeit weeping, but with our heads held high – knowing that we chose to walk with rather than away from Christ. *Soli Deo Gloria.*'

* * *

So far in this chapter we have considered some examples of new congregations that have been formed. In some other cases, ministers have resigned their status and taken up ministry in other denominations in response to the decisions of the General Assembly. The next pages record the personal reflections and testimonies of some of them.

Rev. Ivor MacDonald, Hope Church, Coatbridge (Free Church of Scotland)

For 12 years the Rev. Ivor MacDonald was Church of Scotland minister in Kilmuir and Stenscholl in the north of Skye. As a native of Skye he found it thrilling to preach the gospel to his own people.

Looking back on that period he has written:

'My time there was blessed with gospel growth and harmony in church life. Unlike some congregations, Kirk Session meetings were never an ordeal. Until the latter days voting was unheard of. I counted my elders as friends. Their interests were my interests. So precious was this unity that I made it a practice to remind the people often how precious this was and that we should beware lest Satan cause divisions among us.

'The first indications that there might be fissures in our solidarity appeared in connection with the 2009 General Assembly. I presented an overture from the Presbytery of Lochcarron and

Skye to that Assembly. In the event it was evangelicals claiming the interests of unity who spiked our guns. A proposal for a Theological Commission was put together, happily accepted by the Assembly managers, and approved by the Assembly. The petition included a proposed moratorium on discussing the question of homosexuality. The most immediate result of this was that when I was invited by the Moderator to present the Overture, I was forbidden to address the question of homosexuality. I had been hung out to dry.'

Back in the parish there was huge shock at the events of the Assembly, but with the passage of time, some were convinced that the decisions would have little relevance to them and would not 'trump their commitment to the Church of Scotland'.

After the 2011 Assembly Mr MacDonald intimated to his elders that he could not remain in the denomination but did not wish to leave the congregation.

'In that year Lochcarron and Skye Presbytery passed a motion calling on ministers to consult with their congregations as to whether they were minded to explore change or to maintain the *status quo*. On 29 June we held the first of two congregational meetings to discuss possible future action. It was a tense meeting. I stressed the need for us to stay together as a congregation and floated the possibility of our leaving the Church of Scotland and becoming a Free Church congregation with a minimum of change. I made it clear that if we were unable to stay together as a congregation I would not remain to lead a faction but those who left with me would be encouraged to join with other congregations in the area. Thirty-seven voted to explore change while 27 voted for the *status quo*.

'We held a crunch Kirk Session meeting on 30 August. It was clear that the only way we could remain united as a congregation was to leave together, as some had already intimated that they were going to secede. It was important therefore that the elders gave a lead. However after a very emotional discussion only 3 out of the 9 elders declared their intention to leave.

'Our final congregational meeting on 28 September was an emotional one. The meeting was a watershed. Those who had decided to leave left at this point. On the following Sunday the congregation in Kilmuir Church was reduced by more than half and the elders present were clearly shaken. They had evidently underestimated the strength of feeling of those who departed. I opened the service by reading my demission statement and preached with a great deal of difficulty.

'I endured a difficult month preaching to a greatly reduced congregation and when we finally came to leave the manse in Staffin, my parents, half an hour away in Kensaleyre, took us in to their home where we stayed for the next six months.

'One of the main challenges I faced was to guard my heart from bitterness. There is nothing more damaging to Christian ministry than to be preoccupied with real or imagined injuries to oneself. Many of those who took a contrary view have maintained their friendship with us. I am ready to be reconciled to the few who have not.'

Mr MacDonald has never been in doubt that the General Assembly's decisions left him with no option but to leave the denomination. 'The Lord has been good to us. The trial strengthened us a family and we are now involved in fulfilling ministry in Coatbridge with the Free Church of Scotland.'

Rev. Paul Gibson, Knox Church, Perth (Free Church of Scotland)

At the time of the fateful General Assembly of 2009, Paul Gibson was preparing for ministry in the Church of Scotland. After that Assembly he and his wife Debbie considered prayerfully whether it was right to continue into ministry within the denomination at all, given that the decisions taken by the Assembly had shown such disregard for the plain teaching of Scripture.

However, they still hoped that there might be a reversal of the trend. The fact that many spoke of a growing number of evangelicals within the denomination, plus the reality that the issue of homosexuality in ministry was still to be debated by the 2011 General Assembly, strengthened their conviction that the right thing to do was to continue along the path on which they had been placed in God's providence.

In December 2010 Mr Gibson received a Call from Tain Parish Church. At interview he had responded to questions on how he viewed the situation by speaking openly about the seriousness of the issues and the possibility of a time coming when it might become impossible to continue in the Church of Scotland. He remembers thinking that it was a bold thing to say at such a meeting, but felt that it was important to set out his stall rather than risk being called under false pretences. He was heartened to note that the committee seemed to agree with his position and in due time he was inducted to the charge.

The following Assembly (2011), however, voted to continue on its movement towards the acceptance of those in active same-sex relationships for ordination and to allow homosexuals and lesbians who had been ordained prior to 2009 to move freely between congregations.

For some people, the issue might have seemed distant and even theoretical, but the matter took on a personal and local significance when it came to light that two elders were apparently living together in a homosexual relationship.

Reformed teaching holds that the three marks of the true church are faithful preaching, the right administration of the sacraments, and the exercise of discipline, and in seeking to follow through on the third of these marks, Paul encountered controversy and increasing opposition. He taught that where immoral behaviour is allowed to continue over a prolonged period of time instead of being dealt with in a biblical manner (Matt. 18; 1 Cor. 5), the result is that it will come to be accepted and the minister will be denied one of the means by which he is called to discharge his ministry.

Ultimately, although some members expressed relief that attempts were being made to address the situation, the majority of elders would not support a biblical course of action and in November 2011, Mr Gibson felt that he had no option but to demit his charge.

Two factors convinced him that it was right to leave. Firstly, a clear decision had been taken in May 2011 to move towards the ordination of homosexual clergy which meant that the Church of Scotland had already effectively decided to depart from the authority of Scripture; secondly, the response of several ministers to the situation in Tain left him with serious concerns regarding the nature of evangelicalism within the denomination. Having been advised by some senior evangelicals to just preach the word and 'leave this other stuff alone', he became convinced that the *modus operandi* of many was a detachment of the call to faithfully *preach* God's word from the responsibility of *applying* that word to every aspect of congregational life. There was therefore no option but to leave the denomination.

Paul Gibson is now the minister of Knox Church Perth, a congregation of the Free Church of Scotland. Reflecting on his experience of his life in the Church of Scotland as a member from the age of seventeen, an elder in his thirties, and then a minister of word and sacrament, he has written of three things that lie on his heart.

'The first is a plea: that born again ministers who have, by God's grace, been convicted of the authority and sufficiency of Scripture, would make sure that they are committed to acting upon that conviction – not just in the pulpit, but in doing everything that is in our power to apply its truth within the congregations and denominational settings in which they find themselves.

'My second burden is of thankfulness. God, in his wisdom and sovereignty, allowed me to experience heartache and pain in the earliest days of pastoral ministry and, while no sane person would choose such a situation, it has nevertheless been a sanctifying experience for me to be brought so low in the grace of our good God.

'My final burden is one of prayer. The motivation for church discipline is always a loving desire for the restoration of a person who professes faith in Christ and yet is committed to an ongoing life of sin. It is my earnest prayer that I would be reunited in heaven with those to whom I had the brief privilege of ministering in Tain. However, we know that for spiritual restoration to take place in any life, the grace of repentance needs to be received and exercised. May God grant that grace, both to those who feel trapped in a sinful pattern of living and to those who are called to the privileged task of pastoral ministry and yet so often deny the truths we confess by our actions and our inaction.'

Rev. David S. Randall, Falkirk Free Church

The Rev. David S. Randall tells of being at Crieff Hydro in January 2009 when news came through to the Crieff Conference that the Presbytery of Aberdeen had agreed to induct a homosexual minister to one of its charges. He realised back then that this decision, unless overturned by the General Assembly, would lead to a situation where evangelicals would feel that a line had been crossed, the line of biblical authority, and that it would be impossible to continue in the denomination.

He was inducted as minister of Loudoun Church, Newmilns in March 2009 and found that the General Assembly in May of that year provoked an immediate response in the local congregation. 'Despite a statement from the Kirk Session condemning the decision and distancing ourselves from it, some of our members felt that they could no longer continue – and left either immediately or soon afterwards. They mostly ended up in independent evangelical churches, and included some of our most generous givers. Others resigned their membership but continued attending.

'The Kirk Session met regularly throughout that time, seeking to keep the congregation united and discussing the future, since the elders were unanimous in believing that we neither could nor would be willing to accept the Assembly's decision. For me personally, an incredible amount of time and energy was expended on telephone calls and meetings with fellow-evangelicals – with most of the meetings proving to be frustrating and fruitless, as a result of a lack of clear commitment to action. I was pursued by the Presbytery's Pastoral Oversight and Superintendence Committee because of an article in *Minister's Forum* in which I bluntly stated that the Assembly had departed from the word of God and betrayed not only its calling but its membership. As the result of an apparent abuse of the Presbytery's authority, and bully-boy tactics (where Presbytery sought to have unofficial hearings on unspecified charges) it became necessary to seek legal advice through this process, which ended with no formal charges being made.

'In the spring of 2013 the Kirk Session held a consultation with the congregation to ascertain the level of support for breaking away from the Kirk and seeking a denominational home elsewhere. This was done against a background of active opposition from some long-standing members of the congregation who sought to turn members against their leaders. The consultation revealed that, while a majority in the congregation were in favour of leaving the Kirk, it was only a slim majority – and certainly not a sufficient number of people to sustain a full-time ministry.

'Having done all I could to steer the congregation on a course of biblical integrity, the only option left for me was to demit my charge and status, which I did on 30 September 2013 – ten years to the day since I completed my assistantship and entered the ministry.'

There followed a period of unemployment for five months. On his last Sunday in Loudoun Church, Mr Randall preached on 1 Kings 17 – Elijah and the widow of Zarephath, whose jar of flour was not used up and whose jug of oil did not run dry until the end of the drought. 'It turned out to be prophetic of our experience over the next few months, when our needs (in fact more than needs) were so fully supplied by God, through the generosity of his people.

'On 1 March 2014, I was inducted to Falkirk Free Church, where I have been labouring happily since. Much has happened in our lives (and in the national Church) that could, I believe, have been prevented, had evangelicals been willing to stand together. But God can build his church in ways other than we would choose – our calling is to follow on and to be found faithful, which I now seek to do in a new sphere of service that has opened up.'

Rev. Andrew Downie, Balintore United Free Church

'The elastic finally snapped on Monday 20 May 2013. I had been a member of the Church of Scotland since 1985, an elder since 1989, a Church of Scotland minister since 1991, and parish minister on the island of Benbecula since 2006. I visited my Session Clerk on Tuesday 21 May 2013 to explain and wrote a letter of resignation to the Uist Presbytery Clerk.

'The theological elastic binding me to the Church of Scotland had been stretching for a number of years. The repeated and increasing acceptance of liberal unbelief was disheartening. The 2009 decision of the General Assembly not to discipline a man in an openly homosexual relationship but rather to agree that Aberdeen Presbytery induct him as minister of word and sacrament beggared belief.'

Mr Downie returned from the 2011 General Assembly filled with grief, but determined to continue his resistance. Some members began restricting their giving, specifying their charitable gifts for use only in local ministry and mission. At the June 2011 meeting of Presbytery Mr Downie persuaded Uist Presbytery to issue a statement to all congregations in the Presbytery explicitly refuting the General Assembly decision.

'Then on Monday 20 May 2013 I watched the General Assembly's debate on homosexuality and the ministry via live-stream on the internet. My biggest grief was that the 'facing-both-ways' compromise voted through had been championed by some 'evangelicals'. After five years, with no hint that the Church of Scotland could or would alter its godless trajectory, I could no longer take the stubborn refusal of God's word and will. The elastic had finally snapped.

'The meeting of the Benbecula Kirk Session before morning worship on Sunday 2 June, in which I announced my decision, was an emotional one. The post-service announcement to the congregation was doubly so. I shook hands at the door with tears in my eyes.

'To facilitate handover and to enable our packing, the church agreed to my working three months' notice. Thankfully we had retained our flat in Kilmarnock and my wife and I left Benbecula with heavy hearts on 31 August 2013. It would have been invidious to have formed a breakaway church in a small island community. It was clear that some elders and most of the small, aid-receiving congregation were committed to the Church of Scotland.'

From September 2013 to June 2014 Mr Downie was unemployed. He accepted invitations for Sunday pulpit supply in non-Church of Scotland churches, while praying to the Lord for guidance regarding the future, whether that was in full-time ministry or in secular employment.

'We worshipped happily in Kilmarnock's Central Evangelical Church. The Bible preaching, the contemporary worship, the commitment to prayer and evangelism, the desire for godliness and obedience to God's word, and the loving Christian fellowship all brought huge encouragement. Despite minimal financial income, by the grace of God, these months allowed personal healing and refreshing, both physical and spiritual. Unsought cheques arrived from well-wishers. The Lord provided wonderfully and God's people were wonderfully supportive.'

Then on Sunday 13 April 2014 Andrew Downie preached as sole nominee for the vacant charge of Balintore United Free Church of Scotland, a small seaboard fishing village congregation in Easter Ross. He was inducted on 5 July and is glad to be serving the Lord in his new spiritual home of the Balintore United Free Church.[1]

Rev. Andrew W. F. Coghill, Scalpay Free Church

'When do we leave?' read the text message from Mrs Coghill sent to her husband on 23 May 2011. They had discussed what they would do if the Kirk finally approved homosexual practice amongst its ministers. 'We had lain awake at night wondering how we would survive without home or income, and what would happen to the children.'

'Sermon preparation for the first Lord's Day after the 2011 General Assembly was poorer than it should have been, as so much time and tears went into the drafting of a statement which I read to my congregation, morning and evening, advising them of my intention to demit on 31 August.'

Mr Coghill refers to three different reactions which he found painful. There was the accusation that he was acting with hot-headed immaturity, to which he replied: 'The idea that I would subject my wife and family, to say nothing of the wrench from my parish and people, to such an ordeal *without* having seriously thought through the consequences was (no doubt unintentionally) patronising.'

Others said it was wrong to run at the first sign of trouble, which left him wondering, 'Where on earth has the questioner *been* for the past thirty years? The Assembly decision was not the "first sign of trouble": it was the final straw.'

A third reaction was to accuse him of 'taking the easy way out' to soothe his own conscience, while the hard and faithful thing to do would have been to stay in and look after his flock. In response,

[1] In 2006 the United Free Church and the Church of Scotland entered into a Covenant which recognised each other's ministers and sought to facilitate united worship, ministry and Christian service. However the United Free Church became increasingly concerned about the direction which the Church of Scotland was taking, and in June 2014 the UF General Assembly 'agreed regretfully, in view of the decisions taken by the Church of Scotland, to take steps to bring the Covenant with the Church of Scotland to a close'.

he writes, 'Staying to support the flock is indeed a worthy and laudable vision, and I do not oppose it. The question however might be asked whether we ourselves, as pastors and leaders, are willing to "deny ourselves and take up the cross". Leaving the church of our fathers and mothers is painful.'

The family moved out of the manse on 17 October 2011 after eighteen years. They received many e-mails, letters and cards, including a small amount of 'hate mail', but the majority of messages were supportive and respectful. They included three generous and practical offers of accommodation, one of which, in the Point district of Lewis, was gratefully accepted. The children settled well into school, and they all loved the house and location.

Mr Coghill wrestled with the question of whether or not the Lord might want him to leave the ministry altogether and find a secular job, and admitted to a certain wistful longing for the comparative peace of being an 'ordinary' worshipper in the pews! But he concluded that he was called to the ministry. Had he not been trained for the ministry at considerable time and cost? Do not all denominations need more ministers? To have been *able* to serve but *decline* to do so would be a less than a faithful use of the Lord's resources.

After prayer, he applied for entry into the ministry of the Free Church and this was agreed by its General Assembly in May 2012. But, he says, 'The next six months proved to be a painful and difficult time. I know with hindsight that the Lord wanted me to be in Scalpay, and certainly of all the places I had preached, this was the one where I had felt most peace and contentment; but Scalpay had various obstacles to overcome, not least the lack of an available manse. With most of our worldly goods in storage, with rent and Council Tax, and all the normal family expenses, it was only of the Lord's providential kindness that we survived. We were so grateful to receive periodically anonymous gifts of cash that mysteriously arrived in the post.

'In mid-December 2012 we heard that Scalpay was indeed preparing to call me and in January 2013, the Presbytery Clerk visited us to place the Call in my hands. God is no man's debtor. Each member of our family has warmed to our new home and sphere of labour in Scalpay. The work is incessant at both congregational and presbytery level, but it is all, ALL, the Lord's work. In-service training (compulsory for all serving ministers on rotation) is free of the worldly politicised agendas which blight almost every Church of Scotland event, and the (Free Church) training items are centred in gospel work. The Free Church General Assembly was a pleasure to attend!

'I mourn and pray still for beloved evangelical brethren who suffer yet under the relentless and unforgiving steamroller of aggressive liberalism in the established Church, but each of us must follow our own path of obedience, wherever it may lie. For all the blessings received, I do honestly believe that the best is yet to come.'

Rev. Ross McAskill, Associated Presbyterian Church, Wick

After a background in the APC, Mr McAskill trained for ministry in the Church of Scotland and served in the parish of Knock in Lewis. He resigned after the 2012 General Assembly, was accepted into the APC ministry and invited to move to Wick to do outreach work and oversee a small congregation in Strathy on the north coast. He is thankful for the opportunity to share the truth there. He has communicated these thoughts about 'Evangelicals in the Church of Scotland and Church of Scotland Evangelicals'.

'Like others I had come into the Church of Scotland from another denomination determined that, so long as I could conduct a faithful ministry to the Lord, there was no reason that I should be anywhere else. After all, the Church of Scotland still professed to hold to the authority of Scripture and subordinate to that was the Westminster Confession of Faith. In addition to this I was encouraged to believe that there was something of a spiritual renewal going on in the Church. There were many more ministers who were described as *evangelical* than before.

'However, I became aware that liberalism was alive and well in the Kirk. While there were many in the Church who professed evangelical faith, there was little evangelical influence. Over the years the evangelical tactic had been one of quiet infiltration but it had only succeeded in producing people whose thinking is shaped by the Church of Scotland rather than by the Lord. Evangelicals in the Church of Scotland had become Church of Scotland evangelicals.

'This was evident to me as a minister of a congregation in Lewis (Knock Parish Church) that had enjoyed many years of evangelical ministry prior to my own. Many individuals and congregations persuade themselves that so long as they keep themselves to themselves then they will be faithful. And if there is to be involvement in the wider denomination, the unwritten rule is not to ruffle feathers. This is particularly true of dealings with '121'. I remember a colleague telling me during a particularly difficult issue I was facing in my Lewis ministry that the Presbytery would rather dissolve the pastoral tie than deal with a pressing case of discipline.

'The debacle about the ordination of practising homosexuals demonstrates the depths to which the Church has sunk. This debate has been irksome and as time has gone by it has been evident that change for the better was not likely. This conviction was impressed upon me at the time of the 2012 General Assembly, when after a short debate the Assembly decided to make Church buildings available to non-Christian worship in the name of "Christian charity".

'In 2013 a clear choice was presented to the General Assembly in the debate on the ordination of practising homosexuals. While the truth was openly confessed on the floor of the Assembly, it was an evangelical who put forward the proposal to allow individual congregations to "opt out" of the Church's traditional position and call a practising homosexual minister; that is to say, the Church can remain faithful to the Bible while at the same time being unfaithful to it!'

Rev. Douglas Campbell, Milngavie UF Church

The Rev. Douglas Campbell was dismayed to listen to the debate at the 2009 General Assembly on the induction of a minister who was living in a homosexual relationship. That the debate even took place was a clear indication to him of how far the Church of Scotland had drifted from biblical orthodoxy.

Later in 2009 he was called to serve the congregation of Bo'ness Old. 'Here I followed the evangelical ministry of the Rev. David S. Randall, and although I had the support of the majority of the elders with regard to my position on the issue that had become known as "same-sex relationships and the ministry", the issue became a cause of division within the Kirk Session and congregation. We had some resignations from those holding to the revisionist position as well as from a few holding the traditionalist perspective.'

Some members stopped giving to the Church because they were unwilling to continue to financially support the Church of Scotland; at the same time, they gained several adherents who said that they appreciated the preaching of the word and the worship of God but refused to join because of the denomination's unbiblical leanings.

'After much prayer, Bible-reading, and discussion I came to realise that the crisis in the Church of Scotland was such that I could not in good conscience continue to serve within it. I shared this with a colleague in the United Free Church of Scotland who sympathetically suggested I consider a move to that denomination. Following a meeting of enquiry I applied to the UF Church as a candidate for ministry. Things moved rapidly and I was soon invited to preach as Sole Nominee at Milngavie. I had a clear sense of God's blessing and the Lord confirmed the call to me when the congregation voted unanimously to call me as their minister. And so by the grace of God on 5 March 2015 I was inducted to this charge. I left the congregation of Bo'ness Old with a heavy heart and with my prayerful good wishes, but assured that this new call was of the Lord whom I must obey and honour.'

* * *

We have looked at some examples of new congregations and new ministries. There are also some ministers who have felt compelled to leave the Church of Scotland but who do not fit into these categories. Some, such as the Rev. Roddy MacRae, formerly of Glenelg and Kintail, have resigned and are serving elsewhere – in his case at Rosskeen Free Church – while awaiting guidance about the future.[1] Some ministers have simply retired and departed from the Church of Scotland – for example, Peter Humphris, David Ellis, and John Ferguson. Others have retired earlier than they might have done if it had not been for this controversy; I myself was one of only a handful of ministers without any fixed retirement date. Others again had demitted office for other reasons while being sure that they would have resigned over this issue if they had still been in full-time ministry. The following are some examples.

The Rev. Aonghas Ian Macdonald retired in 2007 after over forty years in parish ministry. He served the congregations of Gairloch (in Ross-shire), Barvas (in Lewis) and Inverness East. In 2012 he left the membership of the Church of Scotland, joined Smithton Free Church in Inverness and is now a recognised minister of the Free Church of Scotland. In explaining why he could no longer remain in the Church of Scotland, Mr Macdonald referred to the vows which he took at his three inductions which he can no longer affirm conscientiously and with integrity. In one he promised to be 'subject in the Lord to [this] Presbytery and to the superior courts of the Church.' He raised the question: Does the phrase 'in the Lord' provide a 'safety clause' that would have allowed him to remain in the Church of Scotland? His answer is that everything turns on the matter of who decides what 'in the Lord' means?

[1] Since this was written, Mr MacRae has been inducted as minister of Helmsdale Free Church of Scotland.

The context of the vows is provided by the 'preamble' which ends with the statement:

> The Church of Scotland holds as its subordinate standard the Westminster Confession of Faith, recognizing liberty of opinion on such points of doctrine as do not enter into the substance of the Faith, and claiming the right, in dependence on the promised guidance of the Holy Spirit, to formulate, interpret and modify its subordinate standards: always in agreement with the Word of God and the fundamental doctrines of the Christian Faith contained in the said Confession, of which agreement the Church itself shall be sole judge.

Although the words about the Church itself being 'sole judge' may carry the implication 'the Church and not the civil power or any other body', Mr Macdonald saw that the phrase could imply that the Church itself (which effectively means the General Assembly as the supreme court and decision-making body of the Church of Scotland) is to be regarded as the sole judge of what is or is not in agreement with the word of God. 'In my view it is doubtful whether as a minister of the Church of Scotland I can claim integrity when I disagree on a major moral issue which I see clearly defined in the Scriptures and still vow my submission and loyalty to a denomination which takes the opposite view. For example, the acceptance of female elders has become mandatory in the Church of Scotland. Those objecting "in the Lord" to women elders and refusing pulpits in the Presbytery of Lochcarron & Skye to a lady Moderator on an official visit were described by a former Moderator at the 2014 General Assembly as "antiquated gangsters".

'In the late sixties, I was in the Assembly when legislation on female eligibility for eldership was approved. It was passed initially with verbal assurances that there would be freedom of conscience for congregations which did not want to go down this route. I heard the late Very Rev. Dr Roy Sanderson, Convener of the Panel on Doctrine, give verbal assurances. Significantly, however, this was not put on official record and a few years thereafter these assurances were dismissed and the new legislation was made mandatory.

'I think it is reasonable to expect this pattern will be repeated with regard to practising homosexuals in the ministry. In a few years' time I envisage similar terms will be used for those who object to the approval and acceptance of same-sex intimacy in the ordained ministry.'

The other vow Mr Macdonald can no longer affirm wholeheartedly in the context of the present debate is 'to seek the unity and peace of this Church; to uphold the doctrine, worship, government and discipline thereof; and to cherish a spirit of brotherhood towards all the followers of the Lord'.

'Fundamentally the unity and peace Jesus prays for (John 17:20-21) is unity based on acceptance of the word of God (John 17: 6b, 8, 14, 17, 20). This acceptance of God's plain word, in my view, does not lie at the core of the doctrine (the teaching on sexuality, etc.) now being adopted by the Church of Scotland. In its declaration of the Church of Scotland's right to be sole judge of what agrees with God's word, how can I, in my disagreement, 'seek its unity and peace; and vow to uphold its doctrine, worship, government and discipline'?

'The issues of "discipline" and "the spirit of brotherhood" are distinguished and defined specifically in 1 Corinthians 5: 9-13, where the immoral person who is committed to such a lifestyle, along with those who manifest lifestyles which promote other vices, is to be excommunicated, according to the apostle Paul, and refused the status of brotherhood rather than being accepted and commended. This, of course, does not imply being disrespectful or unloving toward those who accept such lifestyles or to those of other faiths.

'It is painfully obvious to me that I do not share the view of ministry and of gospel fellowship that is now being defined by the resolutions of the Church of Scotland's General Assembly. The only solution is for me to withdraw from it. I do not believe that this separation involves discarding all contacts with evangelical friends who believe their duty is to continue within the denomination. I may not understand their sense of guidance but I respect them.'

Rev. Thomas Mackinnon was minister at Kilmuir & Logie Easter from 2005 to 2009 and gave notice to the Presbytery of Ross that he would demit his charge on 6 July 2009 following the induction of a homosexual minister to a congregation in Aberdeen. He tells of a dream of arriving at a church to preach and being unable to find a Bible or any book of praise.

'There were some in the Church of Scotland who were concerned that I would be homeless, without any income and with a reduced pension, making the case that I would be foolish to demit due to the financial loss. I can say that I have preached in various pulpits by invitation most Sundays since I demitted, that I have a roof over my head, and am not in debt – other than to the Lord!'

In 2011 Thomas Mackinnon was recognised as a minister of the Free Church of Scotland.

Rev. Dr Bob Fyall was an honorary associate minister at St George's Tron, Glasgow. When the Tron seceded, Dr Fyall resigned as a Church of Scotland minister, and in the following paragraphs he reflects not only on the past but on questions relating to the future of evangelical ministry in Scotland.

'A brief ministry in a difficult and unrewarding Scottish parish was followed by fourteen years in Durham – teaching at a theological college and pastoring a church where 200 to 300 students attended regularly. When I left, the church (then known as Claypath) voted to leave the United Reformed Church so that gospel ministry could continue, as it does today, under the name of Christchurch. So my last months there were concerned with leading that process.

'I returned to Scotland as Director of Rutherford House in 2003 and became involved in a number of bodies; I have been involved in Cornhill Scotland from 1996 until 2015 (part time for one year and after 1997 full time),[1] as well as being an honorary associate pastor at the Tron Church.

'We are in a time of great uncertainty and lack of clarity about the future, but also as evangelicals who have left a denomination which has drifted from its biblical moorings we have great and exciting opportunities ahead of us. One great blessing is no longer having to conform to Church of Scotland training. For a long time the Church of Scotland has handed its training to the University Faculties of Divinity. I know that the Church has a foothold in that training but the drift to liberalism in the Church of Scotland means that few people of evangelical convictions have any voice in the direction and content of training.

'Against this background Cornhill has already proved its worth. In less than a decade a stream of (mainly young) men and women have enriched many churches and benefited from the biblical training received. Cornhill is pioneering the innovative Pastors' Training Course.

'I close with two striking biblical examples of two kings who reacted in different ways. In 2 Chronicles 20, Jehoshaphat, faced with overwhelming opposition prayed "we are powerless against this great force; we do not know what to do, but our eyes are on you". By contrast in 2 Chronicles 26, Uzziah began magnificently but then comes the chilling phrase, "he was marvellously helped until he became strong". Our safety lies in recognising like Jehoshaphat that we are weak and that all the glory is the Lord's.'

Another minister who has felt compelled to leave the Church of Scotland is the ***Rev. Brian McDowell*** who was ordained in the Presbyterian Church in Ireland in 1978. After ministries in Co. Antrim and Belfast, he came to Scotland in 1999 as Chaplain at Fettes College, Edinburgh. In 2007 he was called and inducted to Elie, Kilconquhar & Colinsburgh in the Presbytery of St Andrews.

[1] Cornhill is a training course based in Glasgow which aims to teach the Bible to trainee preachers in order that they can in turn teach it to others. Cornhill also trains men and women to teach the Bible in other contexts, such as youth and children's work and women's ministry.

Here is Brian's own story.

'In 2009 I was appointed as a commissioner to the General Assembly. Upon receiving the papers relating to it I warned my congregation of the seriousness of the consequences attendant on any unscriptural decision regarding homosexual relationships. In the wake of the Assembly's decision I was extremely troubled about my place within the Church of Scotland, but after some discussions and much deliberation and prayer I believed it right to stay within the denomination at that time. However, in the wake of the 2011 decision I believed that I could no longer honour the promise I had made to "be subject to the courts of the Church of Scotland; the Presbytery of St Andrews and the General Assembly".

'I believed that there was a genuine work of God taking place in our three villages and wondered what would happen if I left? Here also I quickly remembered the advice I had given to so many during my years of ministry – leave the consequences of your obedience to God. Through troubled days and sleepless nights my wife and I talked and argued and prayed. Finally we both came to see and accept that integrity demanded we leave a denomination that had, at an institutional level, chosen to set its agenda by the world`s standards.

'There was both relief and deep sadness at this decision. We were going to be leaving a people we had come to love and a work that we revelled in. I am writing this some three years after our leaving and return to Northern Ireland. Although my wife and I have always been at peace about the decision and do not regret it, I have to say that the first weeks and months after leaving were not easy. I have to confess that I was less than Christian in my response. During those first early days I felt some bitterness at the hierarchy within the Church of Scotland. I resented their disdain for the people of the Church, their cynicism about the traditions of this once great Church and, most of all, their rejection of God, his word, and his Son.

'However, as time has passed I have found new areas of service in Co. Antrim, helping in local congregations. This has helped me to see what I believe is a bigger picture. The Church of Scotland has been abandoning God and his word for generations now in many places. The permissive doctrines and elastic ethics it has embraced have resulted in the twin problems of declining numbers and falling finances.

'Deeply sad though all of this is, I believe that there is still hope. God still has his work to do in Scotland and he will not leave himself without a witness in the land.'

Rev. Bob Gehrke was a commissioner to the General Assembly in 2011, along with two elders representing the linked charges of Blackridge and Harthill, St Andrews. He writes,

'I am not one readily given to tears but they were present on that day in 2011 as I sat with two elders in the quiet little chapel tucked away below the University Library next to the Assembly Hall. All three of us were in shock. It was not so much the fact that the General Assembly had voted to openly accept practising homosexuals within the leadership of the Church; it was how the issue was argued: "Yes of course the Bible takes a negative position with regard to homosexual practice but in the light of advances in our understanding, we now know better." We had just witnessed the highest court of the Church of Scotland unambiguously set itself up in judgment of God and his word, and in this matter declared it to be null and void.'

The elders of the two congregations met four days after the close of the Assembly and were unanimous in their declaration that the General Assembly's decision was a denial of Scripture as the supreme rule of faith. They resolved to engage positively with other like-minded congregations in exploring how to unite in standing against the ungodly direction the Church had lurched in. They also planned to make a formal statement to the two congregations and considered how to help members who were unwilling to continue giving to the work of the Church of Scotland. It was decided to take a poll of the congregations to see what level of support the respective Sessions would receive in the event of separation. A paper was circulated and then presented to the respective congregations on 13 May 2012. Almost two thirds of those at worship that day indicated that they would either leave or consider leaving the Church of Scotland unless there was a significant change of direction.

'During the next year it became apparent to the elders that there would be little likelihood of leaving the Church of Scotland and keeping possession of the buildings to which many within the congregations were strongly wedded. The Blackridge elders discussed this difficulty and could see that pursuing separation would result in a painful split within the congregation and also within the village. Although few within the village attended worship, many considered it "their" church. In the face of this, the elders unilaterally decided to discontinue pursuing options and to remain within the Church of Scotland.

'This decision was made toward the end of 2012 making it more difficult for the Harthill, St Andrew's elders. If they were to separate from the Church of Scotland, they would be doing so without the linked congregation and so making it harder to sustain a full-time ministry. Furthermore, like the Blackridge elders, they could now see that it would split the congregation almost down the middle and would mean in effect starting again in terms of material resources. The decision of the General Assembly on the matter however was the final straw.

'On Tuesday 28 May 2013 there was a joint meeting of elders which was scheduled to discuss and respond to the General Assembly's decision on same-sex relationships in ministry. They were disappointed at the idea of a "mixed economy" being accepted, but believed that they would be able to live with the compromise contending that they will always insist on traditional marriage within the Blackridge and Harthill congregations.

'This left me with a decision to make. Throughout the process, I believed it important that I should not push the elders. It had to be their decision – they had to own it because they would have to live with its consequences within their communities long after I was gone. So after speaking to the Presbytery Clerk and the Ministries Council, I announced to the congregation that I would be leaving at the end of June 2013.'

Appendix

The following is a list of ministers who have left the Church of Scotland to the knowledge of the present author. Most have resigned their charges, while others have retired and resigned their status as ministers of the Church of Scotland. A number of others plan to leave sometime in the future. (Note: the name of a minister's last charge is not necessarily identical in time with the date of his leaving the denomination.)

Court, David (Edinburgh: New Restalrig), 2013

Campbell, Donald (Berneray & Lochmaddy, Uist), 2014

Campbell, Douglas (Bo'ness Old), 2015

Coghill, Andrew (Lochs-Crossbost), 2011

de Paula, Alberto (Broughty Ferry: St James'), 2014

Dickson, Peter (Aberdeen: High Hilton), 2011

Dixon, David (Inchbrayock & Montrose: Melville South), 2014

Downie, Andrew (Benbecula), 2013

Ellis, David (UK Director, OMF International), 2013

Fyall, Robert (Associate, Glasgow: Tron), 2012

Gehrke, Robert (Blackridge & Harthill, St Andrew's), 2013

Gibson, Paul (Tain), 2011

Hair, Philip (Edinburgh: Holyrood), 2014

Hardie, Warner (Blackridge with Harthill: St Andrews's), 2015

Humphris, Peter (Inverness: Kinmylies), 2012

Inglis, Donald (Turriff: St Andrews), 2013

Jack, Calum (Stirling North), 2015

Macdonald, Aonghas Ian (Inverness East), 2012

MacDonald, Ivor (Kilmuir & Stenscholl), 2011

Macdonald, John Murdo (Lochalsh), 2011

Mackinnon, Thomas (Kilmuir & Logie Easter), 2009

Macleod, David (Applecross, Lochcarron & Torridon), 2014

MacRae, Roderick (Glenelg & Kintail), 2014

McAskill, Ross (Knock), 2012

McDowell, Brian (Elie, Kilconquhar & Colinsburgh), 2011

McMillan, Andrew (Inverness: Dalneigh & Bona), 2015

Mann, John (Durness & Kinlochbervie), 2015

Martin, Donald (Gardenstown), 2014

Middleton, Jeremy (Edinburgh: Davidson's Mains), 2015

Morrison, Roderick (Glasgow: Gardner Street) 2012

Osbeck, John (Minister to Deaf People), 2011

Patterson, James (Edinburgh: Bristo Memorial), 2013

Philip, William (Glasgow: St George's Tron), 2012

Randall, Andrew M (Larbert Old), 2013

Randall, David J. (Macduff), 2013

Randall, David S. (Newmilns: Loudoun), 2013

Smart, Dominic (Aberdeen: Gilcomston South), 2013

Sydserff, Robin (Edinburgh: St Catherine's Argyle), 2014

Torrens, James (Glasgow: St Rollox), 2011

Watson, Ian (Kirkmuirhill), 2014

New congregations formed in the last few years as a result of Church of Scotland decisions:

Broughty Ferry Presbyterian Church

Chalmers Church, Edinburgh

Christ Church, Edinburgh

Cornerstone Community Church, Stirling

Covenant Church, Newmilns

Drumpelier Christian Fellowship, Coatbridge

Edinburgh North Church

Gardenstown New Church

Gilcomston Church, Aberdeen

Grace Church, Dundee

Grace Church, Kilmalcolm

Grace Church, Larbert

Grace Community Church, Kyle of Lochalsh

High Free Church, Stornoway

Highland International Church, Inverness

Holyrood Evangelical Church

Hope Church, Kirkmuirhill

North Harris Free Church

The Tron, Glasgow

Trinity Church, Aberdeen

West Free Church, Inverness

Bibliography

Books from which I have quoted and which have helped in thinking through some of the issues behind this book.

Sam Allberry, *Is God Anti-Gay?* (Good Book Company, 2013)

A. Atherstone & D. Ceri Jones, *Engaging with Martyn Lloyd-Jones* (Apollos, IVP, 2011)

Roland Bainton, *Here I Stand* (Mentor Books edition, 1950)

I. Barclay, *He is Everything to me* (CPAS Falcon Books, 1972)

ed. Bartholomew, Parry & West, *The Futures of Evangelicalism* (IVP, 2003)

J. Blanchard, *Why Believe the Bible?* (Evangelical Press, 2004)

F. F. Bruce, *The Books and the Parchments* (Pickering & Inglis, 1984)

F. F. Bruce, *The New Testament Documents* (IVP, 1943)

John Buchan, *The Kirk in Scotland* (Labarum Publications, 1985 1st published 1930)

R. Burrows, *Dare to Contend* (Jude Publications, 1990)

R. Burrows, *Signposts From the Past* (Lulu, 2013)

ed. N. Cameron & S. B. Ferguson, *Pulpit and People* (Rutherford House, 1986)

T. Dudley-Smith, *John Stott: A Global Ministry* (IVP, 2001)

Sinclair Ferguson, *From the Mouth of God* (Banner of Truth; revised edition 2014)

J. Fowler, *Mr Hill's Big Picture* (Saint Andrew Press, 2006)

R. Gagnon, *The Bible and Homosexual Practice* (Abingdon Press, 2001)

W. Grudem, *Christian Beliefs* (Zondervan, 2005)

ed. R. D. Kernohan, *The Realm of Reform* (Handsel Press, 1999)

J. G. Machen, *Christianity & Liberalism* (Erdmans, 2009 edition; first published 1923)

A. McGrath, *To Know and Serve God* (Hodder & Stoughton, 1997)

Eric Metaxas, *Bonhoeffer* (Thomas Nelson, 2010)

I. Murray, *A Scottish Christian Heritage* (Banner of Truth Trust, 2006)

I. H. Murray, *Evangelicalism Divided* (Banner of Truth Trust, 2000)

I. H. Murray, *The Life of Martyn Lloyd-Jones* (Banner of Truth Trust, 2013)

A. Orr-Ewing, *Why Trust the Bible?* (IVP, 2005)

J. I. Packer, *Honouring the People of God* (Paternoster, 1999)

J. I. Packer, *Honouring the Written Word of God* (Regent College, 2008)

J. I. Packer, *Taking God Seriously* (IVP, 2013)

J. I. Packer, *Under God's Word* (Marshall, Morgan & Scott, 1980)

Melanie Phillips, *Londonistan* (Gibson Square, 2006)

Melanie Phillips, *The World Turned Upside Down* (Encounter, 2010)

D. J. Randall, *believe it or not* (Rutherford House, 2000)

M. Reeves, *The Unquenchable Flame* (IVP, 2009)

K. Roxburgh, *Thomas Gillespie and the Origins of the Relief Church in 18th Century Scotland* (Peter Lang, 1999)

Beatrice Mair Sawyer, *Seven Men Of The Kirk* (Church of Scotland Youth Committee, 1959)

Thomas E. Schmidt, *Straight & Narrow?* (IVP, 1995)

ed. David Searle, *Truth and Love in a Sexually Disordered World* (Paternoster, 1997)

E. Shaw, *the plausibility problem* (IVP, 2015)

J. S. Stewart, *A Faith to Proclaim* (Hodder & Stoughton, 1953)

W Still, *The Work of the Pastor* (1984; Paternoster & Rutherford House, 1996)

J. Stott, *Christ the Controversialist* (Tyndale Press, 1970)

J. Stott, *Issues Facing Christians Today* (Marshall Morgan & Scott, 1984)

J. Stott, *The Authentic Jesus* (Marshall Morgan & Scott + London Institute for Contemporary Christianity, 1985)

J. Stott, *The Living Church* (IVP, 2007)

ed. D. W. Torrance & J. Stein, *Embracing Truth* (Handsel Press, 2012)

Alex Tylee, *Walking with Gay Friends* (IVP, 2007)

Westminster Seminary Symposium, The Infallible Word (Presbyterian & Reformed Publishing, 1946)

John Wolffe, *The Expansion of Evangelicalism* (IVP, 2006)

David F. Wright, *The Christian Faith and Homosexuality* (Rutherford House, 1994)

ed. David F. Wright, *The Bible in Scottish Life and Literature* (Saint Andrew Press, 1988) ed. David F. Wright & G. D. Badcock *Disruption to Diversity: Edinburgh Divinity 1846 – 1996*, (T & T Clark, 1996)

R. Zacharias, *Cries of the Heart* (Word Publishing, 1998)

F. G. Zaspel, *The Theology of B. B. Warfield* (IVP, 2010)

Index of Scripture References

General Index

Some other books published by the Trust

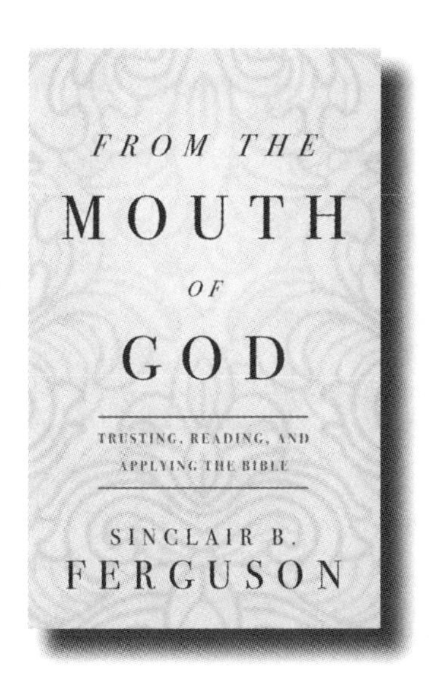

From the Mouth of God:
Trusting, Reading, and Applying the Bible
Sinclair B. Ferguson
ISBN: 978-1-84871-242-3
224 pp. paperback

'A good book for young people and young Christians, probably after they've read Kevin DeYoung's even simpler and briefer *Taking God at His Word*. A great book for everyone else. No matter how mature you are, it will increase your love for and confidence in the Bible, as well as give you some invaluable keys to help you understand and apply it better.' — DAVID MURRAY

SINCLAIR B. FERGUSON
& DEREK W. H. THOMAS

ICHTHUS

*Jesus Christ,
God's Son,
the Saviour*

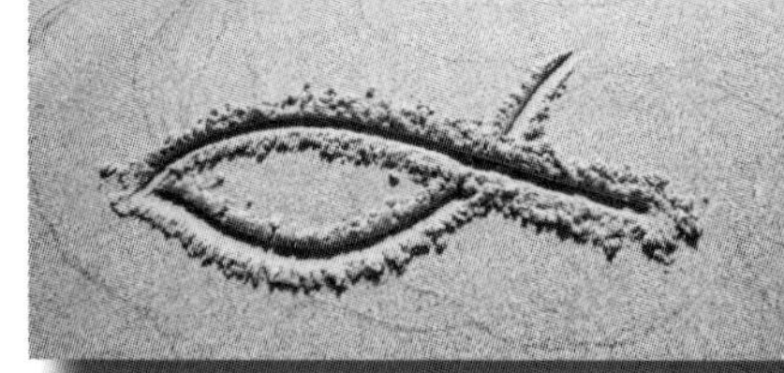

Ichthus: Jesus Christ, God's Son, the Saviour
Sinclair B. Ferguson & Derek W. H. Thomas
ISBN: 978-1-84871-620-9
184 pp. paperback

Ichthus is the Greek word for a fish. Its five Greek letters form the first letters of the early Christian confession that 'Jesus Christ is the Son of God and Saviour.' To draw a fish sign meant: 'I am a Christian.'

To be a Christian, according to the New Testament is to know Christ. But who is he, and what is the meaning of his life? In Ichthus *Sinclair Ferguson and Derek Thomas answer these questions by taking us on a tour of nine key events in Jesus' life and ministry. Their aim is to help us both understand and share the confession of those early Christians who drew the fish sign.*

Ichthus *is a book for everyone and anyone. It will help readers who are already Christians because of what it says about their Master. Those who are wondering exactly what it is Christians believe about Jesus should find many of their questions clearly answered. And those honest enough to admit that they have ignored, or even rejected Christianity but really could not explain what Christians believe about Jesus, will find these pages both clear and challenging.*

Written by two friends who, between them, have been following Jesus Christ for a total of almost a hundred years, Ichthus *will encourage you to share their faith in him.*

Thoughts for Young Men
J. C. Ryle
ISBN: 978-1-84871-652-0
96 pp. paperback

Thoughts for Young Men *is practical, spiritual, and lively. Abounding in advice and good sense, it is still as relevant and helpful in the twenty-first century as it was when it was first published in 1865.*

'Ryle's writings are a distillation of true Puritan theology presented in a highly readable and modern form.' — D. MARTYN LLOYD-JONES

'I see Ryle as a single-minded Christian communicator of profound biblical, theological, and practical wisdom, a man and minister of giant personal stature and electric force of utterance that sympathetic readers still feel.' — J. I. PACKER

A Scottish Christian Heritage
Iain H. Murray
ISBN: 978-0-85151-930-2
416 pp. clothbound

In his book A Scottish Christian Heritage, Iain Murray describes how for 300 years the school of evangelical Christianity changed Scotland as a nation. Passing on the evangel of the Reformation, and growing stronger in persecution, it turned a people to the Bible, and finally gave many of its best sons and daughters to the ends of the earth. For fidelity, joyful perseverance in hardship, and improbable advance, the record remains a witness to the faith that overcomes the world.

'As various recent publications have indicated, Scotland exercised an influence on world history out of all proportion to its size. But the real reason for this has been obscured. It will be found here, however. And in the discovery of it the reader will be introduced to a wealth of little-known literature that is a vital part of the inheritance of the whole Christian church.' — SINCLAIR B. FERGUSON

The Banner of Truth Trust originated in 1957 in London. The founders believed that much of the best literature of historic Christianity had been allowed to fall into oblivion and that, under God, its recovery could well lead not only to a strengthening of the church, but to true revival.

Inter-denominational in vision, this publishing work is now international, and our lists include a number of contemporary authors along with classics from the past. The translation of these books into many languages is encouraged.

A monthly magazine, *The Banner of Truth*, is also published. More information about this and all our publications can be found on our website or supplied by either of the offices below.

THE BANNER OF TRUTH TRUST

3 Murrayfield Road
Edinburgh, EH12 6EL
UK

PO Box 621, Carlisle,
Pennsylvania 17013,
USA

www.banneroftruth.org